EX LIBRIS
Rosina C. Minch

TOOMAS, The Little Armenian Boy

The Avedisian Family

TOOMAS
The Little Armenian Boy

Childhood Reminiscence of Turkish-Armenia

by Dr. Thomas G. Aved

PIONEER PUBLISHING, FRESNO, CALIFORNIA

Jacket Illustration by Edouard Manet, 1832-1883, *The Fifer*.

Illustrations by Margaret Pocock

Library of Congress No. 79-90192
ISBN 0-914330-28-4

It is with boundless love and affection, without reservation, that I dedicate this book to my most beautiful and healthy daughters, Barbara and Laura.

*"Fear not: for I have
redeemed thee, I have called
thee by thy name; thou art mine.
When thou passest through the
waters, I will be with thee;
and through the rivers, they
shall not overflow thee: When
thou walkest through the fire,
thou shalt not be burned; neither
shall the flame kindle upon thee.
For I am the Lord thy God, thy
Saviour."*   *Isaiah 43: 1-3.*

Contents

Author's Acknowledgements

It was my good fortune to meet the author of *Creative Techniques for Christian Writers*, Norma R. Youngberg. She has written and published about fifty books and has taught creative writing extensively. Some of her books have been adopted as standard text books in many schools and colleges. Mrs. Youngberg in turn introduced me to one of her star pupils, Vinnie Ruffo, a protege of undiminished literary ability who also has authored several books and taught creative writing.

It was Vinnie, in collaboration with Norma, who converted my narration from first to third person, and also introduced much of the dialogue in the story.

At the last stage, it was my lovely and beautiful wife Helen who compiled and re-typed the entire manuscript into its denouement.

It is to render to these my profound appreciation and utmost gratitude that I affix my name.

Dr. Thomas G. Aved

CHAPTER 1

Hot Springs in Chermick

"Toomas, look out!" shouted Hovsep. "You almost got your head knocked off." It was like Toomas, thought Hovsep, to want to be first to get under the tree. After an all-morning ride in the increasingly hot sun, the shade of the tree looked cool and inviting.

Toomas drew his horse along the remains of a parapet and sprang down upon it. "Papa, Papa," he yelled with typical 'Toomas' enthusiasm, "there is water coming out from under these rocks!" With that, he threw himself face down upon the grassy carpet and, dipping his head in the cool sparkling water, drank to his heart's content.

It did not take long for the rest of the family to alight from their horses and take advantage of the shade of the huge mulberry tree. Mama Pertoosh soon had spread a tablecloth over a patch of green grass. Six-year-old Toomas, his dark brown curly hair dripping wet around his face and his cheeks flushed red, stood watching his mother and Aunt Nunia place food on the tablecloth—golden brown homemade *chorreg* (yeast rolls) covered with sesame seeds, and delicious goat's milk cheese flavored with parsley. His mouth was watering. He wondered how he could possibly wait another moment to eat as he watched his father and brother Hovsep, four years older, tall and solemn-faced, fill the goatskin with the fresh spring water and bring it to the picnic place.

The Avedisian family bowed their heads while Papa Garabed thanked God for the food and the safe journey. Toomas just *had* to peek while his stomach growled again. He was just looking, he told himself, to make sure Mama had not forgotten the raisins and nuts they would have for dessert.

While they ate their chorreg and cheese, Toomas asked, "Papa, will the hot water at Chermick Springs *really* make your rheumatism go away?" He could not understand how water could make *any* ache or pain go away.

Garabed looked at his young son, who often showed interest in his health. He smiled and twisted his moustache before speaking, as was his custom, and answered, "I hope so, Toomas. I hope it will take the misery away." He touched his hip where the rheumatism hurt the most and grimaced with pain.

He explained, "Our Heavenly Father must have put some healthful minerals in the water and made it very hot so it would be beneficial for aching bodies, for many people say it helps them." Such testimonies had led to his reluctant determination to make this trip to the famous Hot Springs of Chermick.

With the passing of each dusty mile, hope had swelled within the hearts of the weary travelers that this ancient and beautiful place held the cure for Garabed's rheumatism.

"Yes, and we have come a long way," Mama added. It's one hundred fifty miles to the Hot Springs." Her voice betrayed her weariness.

After resting awhile, Papa organized the caravan to move again. He said, "We will arrive in Chermick tomorrow." While he held his hand to shade his eyes from the brilliant sunlight, Mama smiled at him.

What a long caravan it was! Horses and donkeys were loaded down with everything the Avedisian family would need. They had taken enough bedding for their family of four (sister Victoria had stayed in Hini with her own little family) and Aunt Nunia and her frail little daughter Loosig, and of course bedding for the Kurdish escort they had brought with them.

The animals carried rugs, sleeping mats, pillows, blankets and cooking utensils, which clanged as they bounced along. A couple of donkeys carried the food supply that would have to last the journey to Chermick Hot Springs.

Toomas admired his father as he watched him. He was not too young to know that they had been traveling through perilous countryside. He knew that danger lurked behind every tree, hill and mountain. He knew how much the Kurds, a tribe of Turks who inhabited the mountains, hated the Armenians.

Although the balmy spring day had cast a spell of tranquility over the mountains, instant death might stalk the shadows. What if a Kurd sprang from behind a tree, pounced on any one of them and with his dreadful *khandjar* (dagger) sliced off their heads? A shiver slid down Toomas's back.

But Hovsep, he reasoned, had to be right. He had said there was nothing to fear. Their Kurdish escort would be their protection. He was a friendly Kurd, and Papa and Mama trusted him. But could he *really* be trusted?

For the present, however, they had no choice. They *had* to trust him. They had dared not leave Hini without him. Although for hundreds of years the Armenians had lived among the Kurds, they had always been looked upon as strangers in the land.

The Kurds worshipped Allah at the shrine of Mohammed, while the Armenians worshipped God in Christ. The name Armenian throughout the centuries had been synonymous with Christianity. History authenticates that the Armenians were the first to accept Christianity as their national religion, evidenced in 301 A.D. by King Tiridates (Dertad) of Armenia. As intruders in the land of Mohammedanism, they had always been hated.

For three days they had passed hundreds of villages and hamlets where Kurds lived in mud huts. This being strictly Kurdish territory, no Armenian dared make a home here. While the villages seemed peaceful enough in the beautiful green countryside, the mountains were always full of marauding Kurds ready to attack travelers who passed their way.

Sometimes an unfortunate traveler might be held prisoner and a ransom set on his head. Other times the animals would be shorn of their burdens and returned, or the pack and all the traveler's money would be retained as a price for trespassing. In the end, the stranger might even be stoned.

The life of a *giaour* (Christian) had no value in these parts. To do away with the life of a giaour was a most admirable act for a worshipper of Mohammed.

Because these facts had been ingrained within them, Toomas and Hovsep stayed close together. Suddenly Toomas insisted he saw "something" moving behind the tree. "Papa," he said, "what do you think it could be?"

"Don't worry, son. If it is a Kurd in hiding, he will notice our Kurdish escort." Garabed tousled his young son's curly dark hair.

Hovsep had to assure himself as well as Toomas. "Besides, when they hear we are the grandsons of Dada Khazzar and Dada Toomas they will let us go!" Everyone, even the Kurds in these mountains, had heard of the famed grandparents.

Papa was not hurrying the animals but was moving cautiously.

Now they approached another village, comprised of about twenty mud huts which looked like a cluster of giant apiaries, windowless beehives with irregular doors. A dozen dogs raced around the huts, barking. Toomas felt his heart gallop. Would it really be safe to pass through? Then all of a sudden, out of nowhere, it seemed, a man came running down from the mountains to meet them. Toomas was sure he was that "something" that had lurked in the trees. His eyes fell on the dreaded khandjar hanging from the girdle around the man's waist. A young boy about twelve years of age came and stood by the man, a menacing look on his face. He, too, wore a khandjar at his waist. The khandjar was as much a part of a male Kurd's dress as his turban or sheepskin headdress.

The khandjars were usually curved, with beautiful handles made of agate and ivory, inset with precious stones—garnets, turquoises—the most beautiful marquetry imaginable. Carved on the handles were visible notches. Each notch represented the life of a Christian.

Every Armenian knew this painful truth. Toomas rode closer to his mother. Hovsep followed him.

Seeing the Kurd approach, Garabed rode his horse to the front of the caravan alongside the Kurdish escort. The escort held up his hand to stay the approaching Kurd, who looked as though he would just as soon draw his khandjar and get on with his work.

The escort said something in Kurdish. Toomas heard the names "Khazzar and Toomas." Ah! He was telling them they were related to the grandfathers. Would it work?

Hovsep turned, smiling, toward Toomas. "Look, he's telling them who we are."

As the Kurd with the khandjar listened, the menacing look on his face changed to one of recognition. Once again, the names of their wealthy, brave and influential grandfathers had come to the rescue.

For ninety years Dada Khazzar had made himself famous and revered for his generosity, kindness and friendliness towards the Kurds. And Dada Toomas had been a man noted for his dynamic might, a man who knew no fear. His very presence in Hini had many times dispelled any conspiracy against the lives of his many kinsmen. No thief dared to enter his neighborhood. People avoided him, walking around him tremulously. His deep blue eyes spat sparks of fire, and no one looking into them would for a moment choose to be his enemy. Little Toomas had been named after him.

The fame of these two grandfathers had endured. Many times, their names—a password—had saved their lives.

Now the family could travel on to Chermick Hot Springs unmolested. Mother smiled, and as Toomas looked at her sweet face, his fears vanished.

CHAPTER 2

The Cry of War

That afternoon, coming upon a magnificent mountain, they realized they had arrived at the famed village of Argheni. The Avedisians had looked forward in anticipation to seeing the famous landmark, and they stopped for some time to gaze in awe, admiring the picturesque setting. The late afternoon sun shone on its many domes and minarets, transforming it into an emblazoned shrine, incredible in its dazzling Oriental beauty.

The following day the caravan reached its destination. Hundreds of people, lured by the sun and hot springs, milled around. With their horses and donkeys, Toomas's family found a khan, a large two-story building which housed travelers.

The second floor of the khan provided accommodations for people, while the ground floor furnished a place for the animals. Its huge wooden doors swung open to let caravans into the courtyard to load or unload their burdens. A small door within the larger door was for people to go in or out. Toomas couldn't get over the idea of the little door. He ran in and out repeatedly for the fun of it.

The large rustic building, like all the khans, had never seen paint, an unheard-of luxury. The rooms contained no furniture. Guests had to furnish their own mattresses and bedding, for which the family had prepared. It did not take long to unload the animals and settle in the khan.

Another day dawned, bright and beautiful. The sweet smell of new life bursting through the ground after a long winter filled the air. An aura of tranquility seemed to surround the people congregating near the pool, sunning themselves.

Early in the day the family took to their bathing, raptly enjoying a superb, luxurious physical and mental rehabilitation. Already Papa seemed more relaxed as he bathed in the warm spring water. Aunt Nunia wore a happy look as she watched her precious Loosig absorb the sunshine.

Toomas and Hovsep, in the nude, were having a joyous time in the vast octagonal pool with its gallery of cascading fountains in the center of the Byzantine building.

"Come on, Toomas, let's swim across the pool. I'll race you," Hovsep called.

Toomas loved the water and did not need to be encouraged. He wished they never had to go home. He could stay in this place forever. "How long are we going to stay here?" he asked, as he bobbed up and down in the water.

"I don't know. Until Papa's hip feels better, I guess." Hovsep almost swallowed a mouthful of water.

The boys knew there had never been a lack of money. Papa Garabed was a skilled craftsman, store owner and businessman. He had come from a long line of wealthy landowners. They could stay there a month if Papa said so.

After several days had passed Papa had to admit, "The hot springs are really helping my rheumatism."

Pertoosh beamed with pleasure. "Yes, the water is good for everyone's body." Her face, flushed with pink, caused Toomas to think his mother was very beautiful.

Another day arrived. Toomas and Hovsep always left early to get a head start in the pool. They had been splashing, swimming, and pushing each other in glee, when they became aware of a strangeness. The commotion of the many bathers seemed to have come to a sudden halt. One by one, the swimmers began to leave the pool, until the last one had vanished. A strange silence lingered about.

What was the reason? Where had they gone? No one was around, as though the earth had opened up and swallowed them. Only Hovsep and Toomas remained in the pool.

Hovsep came up out of the water for a moment and looked around. "What happened? Why has everyone left?"

"Don't know." Toomas ducked his head under.

Disturbed for only a moment, they continued their splashing and shouting. But something, some sinister thing, had invaded the calm of the pleasure seekers.

All at once, Pertoosh's voice pierced the air, as though coming through a tunnel. "Hovsep, Toomas, come quick, grab your clothes and run! We are going home at once. It is *war!*"

The boys looked at each other and jumped out of the water. "What's the matter with Mama?" Toomas asked. He couldn't understand why her voice sounded hysterical. He had never heard her scream in such a manner. The urgency in her voice was unmistakable.

What did Mama mean? "Hovsep, what is war?" Toomas asked, as he grabbed a towel and hurriedly began wiping himself.

Hovsep gave Toomas a strange look, which said, "Of course you can't know what war is. I hardly know myself." Grabbing Toomas by the hand, not waiting to wipe himself dry, he yanked his brother away. "Come on; something terrible must have happened. Mama never calls like that."

Within seconds the boys reached the khan where Mama waited. War? War? War? Toomas's heart raced. What could it mean?

War! Until that moment the boys did not know the meaning of the word, but in one instant, from their mother's voice they began to understand. And within one short week, Toomas, a six-year-old, was to understand the whole force of the word. War! Even the sun-scorched desert was to come to life. Like lightning the reverberation of the tom-tom beats struck everywhere. War!

In the morning the khan had been filled to capacity, but now, at noon, only three families remained, including Toomas's and the solitary *khanjee* (khan-keeper). The rest had quickly departed for their homes. A few hours before, human voices had sounded like one melodious wave on the surf, but now, like the sea in a dead cave, an ominous dread prevailed.

CHAPTER 3

Hini, a Small Istanbul

The formative years of Toomas's life were spent in perfect contentment and blessedness in Hini, a village in the sanjak of Diyarbekir (Dickranagerd), Western Asia, in a home bequeathed to his father by his forefathers through many generations.

Hini (pronounced high-knee), surnamed *Koochook* (small) Istanbul, was so called because of the mosque with its rounded domes, minarets and surrounding buildings reflecting over the fountain and its resemblance to the famous Saint Sophia Mosque in Istanbul.

As natives of Hini, Toomas's family was called by two surnames. Avedisian meant gospel messenger, and their trade name, Najarian, meant carpenter.

The Avedisian family lived in a comfortable home about a block away from the family stores and the village square. The houses of Hini were huddled together in clusters, adjoining one another, sometimes completely bridging the narrow streets. All the houses had two stories. The first floor of Toomas's house belonged to the animals—sheep, goats, and cows. On the upstairs floor lived the family. Each house faced a different direction. The walls were made of inlaid lumber, held together by stone and mortar. Several times a year Toomas watched as the floors were dampened and slicked with smooth stones to maintain their firmness.

The rooftops, the pride and joy of Toomas's (and everyone's) family, were used all year round for everything from eating and sleeping to playing and entertaining. Toomas would never forget the pleasure and happiness he derived from that warm and comfortable home with its delightful unique rooftop.

The rooftops were constructed of large round beams crossed by twelve-inch boards, filled with soil and sod a foot thick, then rolled and their edges pounded for the rainy season. The houses were built in a square, encircling a garden, insuring privacy. Thus every home had its own sky-roofed garden court.

The Avedisian quarters, part of a four-family complex, consisted of one large living room projecting over the street with a pot-bellied stove in it for heating, and a kitchen with a wood-burning fireplace for cooking. A pantry stored the daily supply of food. This supply always included delicious goat's milk cheese, dry onions, grapes, raisins, apricots, peaches, pears, apples and nuts. Although Papa did not drink wine (nor did he smoke), he kept wine in the pantry for company.

In the basement, the granary room held the family's annual supply of food. Into huge wooden vats, six feet high, went the bulghur wheat, barley, corn and rice. Earthen vessels were also used to hold food.

Once a year, on Christmas, Toomas's father was able to buy a few oranges. These he peeled carefully, cutting them into thin slices which the whole family shared. The peelings were dried and then carefully placed inside folded clothing which was stored in trunks, their fragrance lasting for years.

Hini, for generations home of their ancestors, home of their famous grandfathers, was an irresistible magnet. Very few Armenians had moved away from Hini. Several years back, Pertoosh had bravely defied the advice of the entire village when she decided to send her eldest son, Aghegsanter, to North America to receive an education. Toomas's father, Garabed, came from a family of four brothers and five sisters. Two of his brothers had gone to America to become doctors.

In the complex lived the other two brothers, Amo (Uncle) Hovaness and Ameh (Aunt) Shooshan with their children, Amo Krikor and Ameh Khanum and their children, and Dada Khazzar and Sopig Mama (the grandparents) occupied another apartment. Garabed and his family completed the four-family unit.

Four of Garabed's sisters lived elsewhere in Hini, and Aunt Toomig lived in Diyarbekir.

The Avedisians, a closely knit family, held Dada Khazzar and Sopig Mama as their king and queen. They were fondly referred to in Hini as the "love birds" because of the obvious strong bond of affection between them. They controlled the family wealth, which was one million dollars in houses and lands. They provided for each family's needs.

Toomas thought often of his grandmother, Sopig Mama. How many times had she opened her hand wide, dug deeply into a barrel or crock, and come up with a small amount of raisins or nuts? He had invariably waited with dilated eyes in anticipation of a large amount of goodies, instead of the few that came up within her closed hand.

Sopig Mama, he told himself, was the most wonderful grandmother in the whole world. A tiny woman, her prayers were always long. He could hear her going on and on in Armenian:

"Azdvadz-eem, chem-keederr, gontcheem, gontcheem, intch assem chem-keederr." ("Lord, I don't know, I am always calling. I don't know what to say. Garabed, did you feed the animals? Lord, I don't know. I am always calling. I don't know what to say. Pertoosh, did you cover the children? Lord, I don't know what to say. I am always calling. Hovsep, did you put the mouth of the sheepskin in the water? [This is so that the skin would remain soft, inflatable for pouring.] Lord, I don't know what to say. I am always calling. I don't know what to say. Toomas, did you give water to the cat? Lord, I don't know what to say. I am always calling . . . ")

CHAPTER 4

Saved by the Password

One bright and sunny spring morning Toomas and his brother Hovsep had gone with a group of Armenian boys high up in the countryside near Hini to hunt for *kolobazook,* a delicious edible flower.

Before they had started the kolobazook hunt, Hovsep had tried unsuccessfully to dissuade his little brother from following by taking a circuitous route to the rendezvous with his playmates. As often was the case, he could not be shaken off, and much to Hovsep's chagrin, Toomas became his unwelcome responsibility.

After finding the flowers and eating their fill, the boys hid some in the hems of their garments to take home. All of a sudden, the blissful, fragrant morning was pierced with Hovsep's frantic shouts, "Boys, look! Here come the Kurds!" A gang of boys about their ages was running toward them. Ganging up meant only one thing—the Kurdish boys were going to attack them. Armenian boys knew well of the Kurds' hatred for them.

Luckily, the Armenian boys had become experts in the only art of self-defense that they knew. Hovsep and his friends reached into their pockets for the supply of stones that each carried, and quickly unfastened the colorful slingshots which they wore around their waists like sashes.

"Look!" cried Toomas, in a shrill voice. "There's another bunch of them coming!" With the advantage of numbers, the Kurdish boys came closer, jeering and challenging. They seemed to appear from everywhere.

Seeing that the odds were against them, Hovsep yelled, "Come on, let's run!" Every boy ran for his life, even little Toomas, but being the youngest, he could not run as fast as the others. He was so frightened, he was almost sure that the Kurds would reach him first and stone him to death.

Hovsep turned to see if his little brother was keeping up. "Hurry, Toomas, run faster!" he called, but Toomas's little legs could not propel him any faster, no matter how hard he tried. Realizing that his little brother could not possibly keep up, Hovsep turned to go back to help him.

By now the Kurdish boys, stones in hand and vengeance in their eyes, had surrounded them. Breathless and exhausted, Toomas stopped running, his heart pounding wildly. What would happen now? The two boys turned and faced the running horde of boys about to descend upon them. As they stood there, galvanized on the spot, they noticed that the Kurdish boys, too, had suddenly stopped in their tracks. Their leader advanced slowly toward Toomas and Hovsep, a strange look of surprise on his face. Toomas, too terrified to look, clung to Hovsep's leg. The other Kurdish boys looked on with interest.

The Kurdish leader said, "Tohrreh Kerva Khazzar, Kerva Toomas!" (You are the grandsons of Khazzar and Toomas!) All his deviltry vanished instantly. He broke into a laugh. "Lucky for you that you are the grandsons of Khazzar and Toomas! We would have buried you under a hail of stones."

Toomas heard the words and released his hold on Hovsep.

Hovsep was saying, "Yes, yes, they are our grandfathers." But Toomas, too stunned to speak, just gasped with relief.

"Come here," the leader ordered Toomas. He would not release them without first searching for any booty in their pockets.

A wave of reluctance swept over Toomas. One pocket was full of dried mulberries, which to him were as luscious a treat as any piece of candy. In the other pocket he carried a treasured red handkerchief and the tiny New Testament his parents had given him for his third birthday. Although he could not read, he loved to open the Bible and just mouth the letters of the words. He reached into his pocket and fingered the little book.

As the leader searched his pockets, Toomas's eyes filled with tears. He said, "Please don't take my handkerchief." The Kurd found the mulberries and helped himself to every last one. Then he found the little Bible, but did not seem interested. Toomas knew that he did not recognize it as a Christian book. Then he put Toomas's red handkerchief into his own pocket.

"Ha," he boasted. "You are lucky you are still alive!" His voice was filled with jubilance. He seemed content with his booty. Hurriedly, he searched Hovsep's pockets and relieved him also of his berries. Hovsep did not protest.

Afterward, Hovsep reached for Toomas's hand. "Let's go," he said. When they had gone a few feet, he scolded, "Come on, stop your crying. We can always get more mulberries."

In his heart Toomas knew Hovsep was right, but oh, how he hated to part with his luscious berries and, especially, his cherished red handkerchief. He would never forget this day.

CHAPTER 5

Home

The boys hurried back to Hini, home and security. Hini, the most beautiful spot in the world, they thought. A precious gem in a lush green valley surrounded by lofty mountains with crystal clear springs.

The Avedisians were one of the wealthiest families in Hini. They owned all the administration buildings overlooking the large fountain in the heart of the village. They owned the only school building in Hini, store buildings, many houses and lands. These lands yielded corn, rice, wheat, barley, fruits, and vegetables.

As the boys neared home, they could see the center of the village with its ancient fountain containing six large tunnel-like chambers dispensing cool clear spring water the source of which no one knew. This fountain measured some one hundred feet square and was surrounded by a thick stone parapet about three feet above the street level and fourteen feet above the water level. Steps led down to the water, and here the village housewives came daily to carry the sparkling water in fancy colored pots back to their homes. Some filled sheepskins and let the donkeys carry the load.

Toomas often saw the Kurds, after performing their religious ablutions at the fountain below, come to perch on the flat surface of the wall and commune with Allah, with many gestures.

On hot summer evenings, Toomas, Hovsep, and the other village boys, unable to resist the temptation, dared to jump into the water naked. If one heard footsteps, he would yell, "There's someone coming. Quick, let's run!" Grabbing their clothes, they would run as fast as they could.

In the middle of the cobblestone street, between the fountain and the government buildings owned by the Avedisians, stood two stately mulberry trees which yielded luscious large white berries about two inches long. Toomas loved those berries, but the Kurds considered them their own private property and kept a constant vigil to keep the Armenian boys from eating them.

One day Toomas sneaked up in one of the trees, and as he ate contentedly of the sweet fruit, all at once, without warning, a barrage of stones came hurtling toward him. He had to think quickly. What should he do? Should he climb down under the hail of stones and run home with blood trickling down his face, or stay in the trees until it got dark, or until the Kurds ran out of stones?

He decided to stay in the tree, but climbed higher and clung to the thick branches until the darkness of the night arrived to save him. Then he ran for his very life, and once safely at home told his worried mother about his brush with near disaster.

In the business district of Hini, beneath the balcony of Papa's store, every local festivity took place. On these merry occasions and *only* at these events, a sense of friendliness developed between the Kurds and the Armenians.

During these times the Armenians helped to celebrate the Kurds' *Ramazan* and *Bairam* (their month of religious fasting). The Kurds, in turn, helped the Armenians celebrate their *Vartavar* (festival of roses). This Christian feast commemorates the transfiguration of Jesus on the mountain, when, as he prayed, Moses and Elijah appeared. It comes fourteen weeks after Easter.

At this feast of Vartavar, the Armenian people decorated their churches with roses and flowers and let white pigeons fly outside the windows of the church. The feast was never allowed to end without the joy and thrill of *rashesh*. Everyone, children as well as grownups, looked forward with the highest anticipation for the time of the rashesh, when they literally threw water at one another with anything hollow enough to hold water. Toomas and the other children thought rashesh was the best part of Vartavar. What fun, to sprinkle water on each other!—something they were not always permitted to do.

On these infrequent feast days when the Kurds and the Armenians mingled as friends, hatred, grudges and racial prejudice were forgotten. Mother Pertoosh would say, "Oh, that God's love would fill people's hearts so that there would never be any hatred, and that all would always get along as we have today." She would mingle among the Kurds graciously offering the delicious foods she had prepared for the day.

Toomas's family loved these times when everyone was happy and hatred seemed to vanish. Laughter was everywhere. Toomas and Hovsep loved to watch the men dressed up in their Sunday best—brightly colored shirts and wide pants—parading and singing and dancing in the streets. The band played on their *dawools* (large bass drums) and *zoornas* (instruments of the oboe family). The children and grownups marched after them, singing and clapping their hands.

Toomas did not know which he liked best, Vartavar or Easter. On Easter Sunday every boy and even most of the men brought colored boiled eggs, hidden in their pockets, to church. After the services, as was the custom, they congregated in front of the church, took the eggs out of their pockets, and began a game of egg playing. Only those who were experts could play eggs. Toomas was proud of his big brother Hovsep and he watched with envy as Hovsep began by tapping both ends of an egg on his forehead to test its strength. Then he would strike an opponent's egg with his own, while the opponent exposed only a small area of one end of his egg between his thumb and forefinger (the smaller the exposed area, the more to his advantage). The one who succeeded in breaking the other's egg would get to keep it. The bartering went on for hours. Hovsep taught Toomas how to play and often they came home with their pockets bulging with colored Easter eggs.

Harvest Time

Dear to the hearts of Armenians was the harvest time. Songs of happiness were on everyone's lips—fathers making preparations, women and children laughing. Toomas and Hovsep loved harvest time and the excitement that went with it. All business was at a standstill. Stores were closed, streets deserted. All the villagers were out reaping their harvests, laying up the year's annual provisions in their cellars. What a happy time this was! During this vintage time, every family moved into its own vineyard to harvest the grapes. The vineyards were located anywhere from one to five miles outside the village and were fenced off by limestone walls which had been loosely thrown together. Nearly every family owned a vineyard; some owned several.

The Avedisian family, like other families, never sold their crop. It was cultivated in its entirety for the sole purpose of providing raisins, wine, and mouth-watering delicacies for their family.

Within each vineyard stood a cobblestone hovel which served as a shelter. These hovels, rugged and ramshackle, were more like caves without doors or windows. They required yearly repair and sometimes actually caved in on their occupants. Their very ruggedness made them fun and exciting for the children.

Near the hovels were stone troughs which were about eight feet square and six feet high. These were for the purpose of crushing grapes. At the end of each trough there was a hole to let the crushed grape juice run out. Beneath the hole was a smaller trough which held a container to catch the juice. Frequently Toomas's mouth was there to catch it, whetting his appetite for sweets.

Families joined together to help each other pick the grapes. Fathers, mothers, brothers, sisters—everyone carried a wicker basket according to his size. As they picked the grapes and carried them to the troughs, they laughed, sang, whistled and talked. What fun to do things together as a family!

Because grape-crushing was considered a hard job, husky men, usually Kurds, were hired to crush the grapes. After thoroughly washing his feet, the crusher would stomp back and forth over the grapes in the troughs,to extract the juice.

The juice was poured from the pans which caught it into huge copper kettles. The kettles were placed over an open fire and the juice boiled. It had to be stirred constantly and watched carefully, lest the bottom scorch, and it had to boil throughout the night. Both men and women took turns stirring. Pertoosh used a wooden ladle which Garabed had made.

To make a delicacy called *bastegh* (a kind of fruit leather), the boiled liquid was poured into large pans. Pertoosh and Victoria then poured the liquid from the large pans into smaller pans, to cool it. Holding the smaller pans as high as their heads, they then poured the contents into pans sitting on the ground. Each time the process was repeated, the juices became cooler. To give the liquid a lighter color, they added white wood ash.

This liquid was then poured back into the large copper kettles for more boiling. The women continued to stir constantly, and after it had boiled down they added flour gradually to obtain the desired thickness.

The next step was to spread special clean white sheets (about three feet by six feet) across dry vine prunings, which had been saved for this purpose. Pertoosh, who was an expert at it, carried the boiled, thick liquid in scoops and poured it over the sheets, spreading it evenly to obtain a paper-thin thickness. Sometimes nuts were sprinkled over the juice.

After drying in the sun for several days, the sheets were turned over and dampened, which allowed the layer of purple confection to come loose. Now the mouth-watering and delectable bastegh was finished. The entire family joined in to fold over and over the long sheets of transparent grape confection until only a small square or triangle remained. This delicacy served as candy for the children and adults, since candy was unknown. Stored in a dry place, it kept for a long time, perhaps a year or so.

Another type of confection Toomas's mother made from the grapes was *kesma*. The thick juice was spread on sheets to a thickness of one inch. Then coarsely ground nuts were sprinkled generously over the grape juice. After drying, it was removed and cut into diamond shapes or squares.

The king of confections, however, was *takavoragon rojig*, commonly known as *sujough.*

First, Pertoosh would soak almonds, walnut halves or sweetened apricot seeds overnight in water, to prepare them for the process of dipping. The softening would prevent the nuts and seeds from breaking when a needle was threaded through them.

After being threaded on strings about two feet long, they were allowed to dry before being dipped. Once dried, five strings of nuts were fastened, wide apart so they wouldn't touch each other, to a wooden arm. Then they were dipped into the thickened lukewarm grape juice repeatedly, just like candles. Pertoosh was

very careful to keep the juice in the kettle at the right consistency and temperature. She dipped them three times to get the desired thickness. The strings with the coated nuts were then dried in the sun, and when thoroughly dried were ready to be stored away. Toomas often helped his mother, and could hardly wait to eat some.

After much test-tasting, all of these delectable confections were placed in large earthenware vessels, sprinkled with flour, and sealed for winter use.

These vessels, and huge wooden vats filled with rice, whole wheat, cracked wheat, barley, corn and other foods from the harvest, were stored in a cool, dark basement room. Large gunny sacks full of shelled almonds and walnuts and dried fruit from the family orchard were also stored in this room, adding to the annual provision of food.

Every family was involved in the preparation of the staple food *ka-woor-ma* (lamb meat). Garabed brought a dozen or so whole lambs from the slaughterhouse to make the ka-woor-ma. He cut the meat into two- or three-inch pieces which were placed in a large copper kettle and cooked in their own fat over an open fire for long periods of time. So that the bottom would not scorch the women stirred the meat with long wooden ladles.

After it had been sufficiently cooked and had cooled off, the lamb was poured into various-sized crocks and used as needed during the entire year. Cooked in this manner, it never spoiled.

These morsels of meat—ka-woor-ma—were most delicious when cooked with pilaff, either rice or bulghur (cracked wheat). They were also delectable fried with eggs.

Near the end of what was to be the last of these happy harvest times, Pertoosh sat down to rest for a moment, and as she rested she watched Garabed working in the vineyards and the children skipping and frolicking. She was thinking, "How blessed am I! Such a wonderful husband, good home, all the food we can eat, and four lovely children!"

Looking around her, she saw Toomas and Hovsep race merrily by, following some other children. "Little Toomas," she smiled to herself. "How much you are like your father!" Small and wiry he was, with his father's large brown eyes that could melt your heart, and light brown hair with large curls that fell into his face. She wished that she had half of Toomas's energy. He was always busy, always curious, never still. His busy hands and curious mind too often caused him to get into mischief, or to be scolded and reprimanded by Hovsep. Hovsep, she thought, taller and older, with thoughtful eyes, seemed to look right through you. His hair was darker and more wiry than Toomas's. Hovsep was the quiet one, the reader, and the busy Toomas often seemed to try his patience almost beyond endurance. As a result he often scolded Toomas and sometimes pummeled him, trying to break his indomitable will, though at the same time he loved his little brother very much.

Pertoosh and Garabed's marriage had been blessed with six boys and two girls. Death, however, had taken half of them, leaving Aghegsanter, Victoria, Hovsep, and Toomas, the youngest.

As Pertoosh sat there reminiscing, she could hardly contain herself with the happiness she felt.

Later in the evening, after the day's work was finished, bonfires were lit and the men tried to outdo each other spinning their adventurous tales, told and retold for centuries, especially the whimsical anecdotes of Nasr-ed-din Hodja. How the children listened, wide-eyed and rapturous, until gradually they fell asleep to the singing of Armenian ballads and dancing. And thus ended another day of another bountiful harvest season.

CHAPTER 7

Fun Time

Living at its best took place during the summer months when Armenian families practically lived on their rooftops. The happiest, most longed-for moments, the "ultimate of living," Toomas thought, came on summer evenings.

For each family on its own rooftop, supper became a picnic, and the Avedisian family was no exception. Up and down the ladders went the children and adults carrying sleeping mats, cushions, rugs, tablecloths, food, water, glasses and utensils. A tablecloth was spead on the floor and the family sat around it. A large bowl holding the main course was placed in the center. Each member dipped into the dish with his spoon (carved from wood by Garabed). Sometimes half a dozen spoons converged upon the bowl at the same time.

After the evening meal, the real fun began. There would be group dancing to Armenian folk songs, with singing and hand-clapping, and sometimes the accompaniment of the dawool and zoorna. The men told hair-raising stories of their heroic deeds and of their encounters in the mountains with formidable savage brigands, Tartars and Chachans.

All this merriment took place in the moonlight, without any artificial lights. On these memorable nights of beauty, laughter and love, as friends visited one another from roof to roof, the Asiatic moon floated across a silvery sky, bathing the surrounding mountains with its radiance.

The beds were sleeping mats, carried up earlier in the evening by Papa and Hovsep, and spread out on the floor, or on a portable *takht* (a wooden platform which held several mattresses and had corner poles which would support a sheet to encircle it for privacy). While rooftop sleeping held its own special delights, it was not a safe experience for those who walked in their sleep.

Sometimes the rain would come, sending everyone scurrying down the ladder in the middle of the night. Toomas and Hovsep found the rain delightful. Sheets, pillows, rugs, mats, and night-shirts would go flying through the air while the children jumped on the heaped bedding. What fun it was to head for the veranda below!

Frequently the fun of the night was interrupted by a piercing cry, *"Dah-ron! Dah-ron!"* ("Thieves! Thieves!") Again and again, while family merriment went on on the rooftops, Kurds would enter the houses below and do their looting—perhaps a pair of shoes, a coat or shirt, or a wooden bucket. One night Toomas awoke as his bed cover was being yanked away, but by the time anyone could give chase, the Kurds were beyond shouting distance with their stolen prize. While looting by Kurdish peasants was common, no Armenian ever thought of looting a Kurd's house.

During the daytime, rooftop play furnished many hours of sheer delight to every Armenian child. The grouping of the houses made the rooftops a natural playground. All games and sports, even those requiring running and jumping—or digging shallow holes with wooden sticks—were played on the rooftops.

A favorite game of Toomas and the other little ones was "jumping the shoes." The object of the game was to jump, bare-footed, one foot at a time, on top of the loose-fitting house-slipper

TOOMAS
The Little Armenian Boy

*Childhood Reminiscence
of Turkish-Armenia*

by Dr. Thomas G. Aved

following years. This beautiful and unfor-
gettable story is filled with laughter and with
tears, with testimony to the power of prayer,
and the value of a well-disciplined and
healthful life. You will love the ambitious,
curious, energetic little Toomas and his
loving family, and will smile with them and
cry with, and for, them.

The author, a retired physician, is a
Seventh Day Adventist and a strong pro-
ponent of healthful living. He learned the
fundamentals of taking the best care of his
body when he was young, and has never
forsaken them.

Although the story told in this book is not
the story of today's Toomas, it is interesting
to find out where the events of his boyhood
led him as the years went by. The most
unusual fact of his later life was the invention
of an exercise which he calls the single-leg
pushup, a feat he has often performed more
than 300 times in a row, and at which he has
never been excelled. In fact, no one else has
ever been able to do it! His demonstrations
are always inspiring and challenging to
young people—and to older people, too.

It will be no surprise to the readers of this
book that the resilient, determined little
Toomas grew up to be such a man.

type shoes that were placed a distance apart. The frequent sliding and falling only made it more fun!

The biggest thrills came from watching Hovsep and the older boys jumping from one rooftop to another, especially from a lower roof to one several feet higher. Toomas wished his legs were longer so he could join them.

Climbing the moveable ladders that stretched to the rooftops provided its share of fun for the children. When not in use, these ladders were either turned sideways and hooked against the walls, or taken down completely. If they were hooked against the walls, the barefooted boys would climb them sideways, anyway, in their daredevil antics.

Another game played frequently was *chanch*, played with two sticks. One stick, two feet long, had a pointed end. The other was four inches long and both of its ends were tapered to a point called *chanch*. The purpose of the tapering was so that when it was placed on the ground and hit on either end with the "batting" stick, it would flip up in the air, to be struck at with the "bat." Hovsep was good at chanch, and promised to teach Toomas to be as good.

The most popular game played by the boys was *jon*. The jons were sesamoid bones taken from the ankles of sheep. They were cleaned, polished, and treasured, and the best-looking pair was selected by an expert jon player to be used as his shooting or leader jons. Sometimes they were painted different colors and their centers leaded for effect. Almost every boy carried a pair of leader jons in his pocket. These were used in games much as marbles are now used. Sometimes walnuts, almonds, or apricot seeds were used instead of jons.

While the children played, Pertoosh was busy at her many tasks. When Toomas could smell the fragrance of baking bread, he knew Mama was making chorreg.

Another task was candle-making. Pertoosh was an expert candlemaker. She melted tallow and beeswax or mutton fat in pans to the desired thickness, and enlisted Toomas and Hovsep to pull long strings through it, in fifty- or sixty-foot lengths. After cooling and hardening, they were rolled and twisted in pocket sizes, to be used for lighting.

When not in use, the bedding was stacked up in a bed alcove in the Avedisian's living room, almost touching the ceiling, then covered with a huge tapestry of beautiful design.

Sometimes, in the evening at bedtime, when prolonged company had not taken their leave, sleepy-eyed Toomas would climb on top of the pile and go to sleep.

Other times, while playing, Toomas and the children would climb on top of the pile and hide. Suddenly, accidentally-on-purpose, they would fall, toppling the bedding to the floor in an avalanche. When Mama or Papa scolded, they would insist they were only bringing the bedding down for the night.

To Armenians, a living room was literally a *living* room. The family, when not on the rooftops, slept, ate, and played there. No furniture cluttered the room. At mealtimes, the tablecloth was spread over the rug on the floor (as it was on the rooftop) and the family sat around it to eat. Cushions took the place of chairs, and mats with pillows behind them, lined against the wall, provided a place to relax.

Sometimes, in this all-inclusive room, at mealtimes table legs hinged together at the center were placed on the floor and covered with a round table top. When not in use, this table was put away. The table legs, Garabed's handiwork, were a foot high and had been shaped on a lathe with ornamental scroll work.

For napkins, a long piece of cotton cloth with a fringe of ten to twelve inches circled under the table.

Much space existed between the ceiling and the round beams extending across the porch of Toomas's family complex. Therefore, strong ropes were hung through the beams for hammocks and swings, and the entire family enjoyed swinging as a pastime.

Also hung from the ceiling were sheepskins filled with goat's milk ready for churning. Toomas couldn't get over the magical idea of the animal skin making butter and cheese by being churned.

Birds of many colors found the ceiling a sanctuary for their nests and stayed the year round. Often Toomas would swing for hours, listening to the birds singing and attempting to imitate their melodious songs by whistling.

The ceiling spaces also furnished a place for the family's beehives. Since honey was their main sweetening agent, they produced their own. Four large cylindrical beehives made of clay were suspended from above. Pertoosh extracted the honey, a task demanding that she live up to her name, which meant "intrepid." With a round sieve in front of her face and a shawl wrapped around her head, she went bravely to the job. Toomas always marveled at his mother's lack of fear.

CHAPTER 8

Garabed Tells Stories

On cold winter evenings the family nestled together in a circle around a *monkul* placed either on the floor or under the *koorsee*. A monkul was a square metal pan about two feet wide, with four legs, about six inches high, to support it. It looked like a miniture bathtub and was filled with hot cinders.

The koorsee was a large square low table over which Toomas's mother spread a heavy woolen quilt that reached to the floor. The family sat around it with the warm quilt tucked up to their waists while they ate, played games, sewed or knitted. What fun little Toomas and his cousins had playing hide and seek under the koorsee!

It was also a fine place and time for story-telling. Many were the tales spun by Papa and the other elders while the children listened, utterly enthralled. One of the favorites was the story of Toros. Papa would twist his long moustache, look around to be sure everyone was listening, and begin:

"Toros was our church custodian, a long-time unmarried man whom everyone loved and had fun with. But it seemed that Toros possessed a dual personality. On Sunday morning he would strike the huge metal bar suspended in the steeple of the church with a steel hammer in each hand, to invite people to worship. When Toros struck the bar with such forceful authority, no one dared to stay away. Toros gloated over his authority. Yet he was very naive and very simple. He believed everything that anyone said. He often said that he would like to be translated to heaven without experiencing death.

"One dark Saturday night a group of young men schemed to help him achieve his wish. They climbed unnoticed into the steeple of the church and extended a long rope down to the floor of the sanctuary. Then they cried with muffled voices, *'Toros, Toros, oor es?'* ('Toros, Toros, where are you?')

"'*Aha, hos em, Der im, hos em!*' ('Here I am, Lord, here I am!') exclaimed Toros with a trembling, fearful voice.

"'Toros, take this rope and tie it around your waist. You're going to be translated.'

"'No, Lord, no. I am not worthy, not worthy!' Nevertheless, he tied the rope around his waist. The pranksters then pulled him up to the dome and tied him there to dangle all night. On the following morning when the worshippers entered the church, they saw Toros desperately swinging in the sanctuary.

"'Toros, what are you doing up there?' they asked in disbelief.

"'Those bad boys played a trick on me!' answered the trembling Toros."

This made Toomas and the others laugh with glee.

Another tale that Garabed loved to tell was how he and Pertoosh had become engaged when she was only twelve years old. "How well I remember the tragedy that almost tore us apart. One day shortly after our betrothal, as your mother Pertoosh sat on a bench in her kitchen knitting, her mother (Yeghisapet) announced, 'Garabed has come to visit. Go to your room.'

"It was the custom that a fiance should not see his betrothed, so I went to visit not Pertoosh, but her parents. And if by chance Pertoosh would be where I could see her, she pulled her silk shawl over her pretty face and quietly stood still or sat down until I walked by. I, in turn, was a gentleman and turned my head, pretending I had not noticed her.

"The shawl, of course, couldn't stop the pitter-patter of her heart," he said, as he smiled charmingly across the table at her. Then he continued, "This time, she laid her knitting needles on the seat and hurried to her room to beautify herself, intending to come and place herself in my full view, hoping I would notice her!

"When she returned, she had forgotten the needle and sat directly upon it. 'Oh, oh!' she cried out, for the needle had pierced her in a most tender spot. Trying not to cry, she pulled the needle out, and feeling dizzy, leaned upon the fireplace mantel. Suddenly she fainted, falling face down into the smouldering ashes!"

Breathlessly, the children waited for him to continue. "Not knowing what had happened to my sweetheart, I visited with her parents and left. When her mother entered the kitchen, she found Pertoosh lying on the hearth, her face buried in the fireplace. Of course, no one knew how long she had lain there.

"'Toomas!' her mother screamed. (That was Dada Toomas.)

'Come quick. Pertoosh has fallen into the fire!' Together they pulled her out of the fire.

"Horrified, her mother cried, 'Oh, Toomas, what shall we do? Look at her face!' Already her face was a mass of fiery redness.

"'Stay with her. I will go and kill a lamb,' her father commanded. Since there were no doctors in Hini, people always knew what to do in case of an emergency.

"Wasting not a moment, her father went and slaughtered a young lamb, skinned it, and wrapped the raw skin around Pertoosh's face. For weeks she wore the wool-faced mask over her raw, burned face."

Garabed continued, telling the wide-eyed children, "Your mother worried whether she would ever be the same again. If her face had lost its beauty, would I still want to marry her? Her mother tried to comfort her, but for awhile she was inconsolable.

"To make matter worse, her parents said to me, 'Garabed, we are not sure that Pertoosh's face will ever be the same, or that she will not be blind. Therefore, you are free to break your engagement.'

"'No!' I shouted. 'I love Pertoosh. I want her only, to be my wife.'"

Papa smiled at Mama as he looked at her out of the corner of his eyes, savoring with delight the attention of all eyes upon him. Twisting his moustache, he went on.

"'Are you sure?' her father asked me. 'You are young and may later change your mind.'

"'I am sixteen years old, and know my mind! I want to marry Pertoosh as soon as she is well.'

"I had made up my mind. And when Garabed makes up his mind, no one can change it!" With this he brought a clenched fist down on the table. The children all heaved sighs of relief and smiled at one another. Then he continued.

"Hearing the news, Pertoosh rejoiced and recovered in a most amazing manner. Her face retained its smooth and velvety look. The joy in her heart reflected in her eyes. She was determined not to allow this experience to ruin her life, and she has made me the happiest man in Hini!"

As Toomas looked up at his mother busily sewing, he thought she was the most beautiful mother in the world.

Garabed and Pertoosh were married shortly after the near-tragedy, and happiness filled their lives. But seven long years passed and though they longed for a child, none came to bless their union. Like Hannah of old (in the Bible), they turned to God, promising that if He gave them a child they would dedicate him for His cause. God heard their prayers, and after Aghegsanter, their firstborn, came of age, they kept their promise to dedicate him to God, and sent him to America with his grandmother Yeghisapet and her six daughters. Aghegsanter was to become a minister in America.

CHAPTER 9

Garabed and the Devils

Pertoosh, blessed with more than her share of courage, had found her match in Garabed, her husband. He possessed unshakable will power.

Having made up his mind that smoking and drinking were sins, he determined that these vices would never touch his lips. He would say, "I can't see Jesus with a glass in his hand puffing on a cigarette in his mouth."

His father, Dada Khazzar, smoked occasionally and the children helped him roll cigarettes. But not Garabed. Never!

Some of his friends, well aware of his abstinence, determined once to break his will.

One evening the family took their lantern to guide them through the narrow, winding, unleveled streets, and made their way to a friend's house, as they often did. Other families had gathered and were already dancing and playing games and drinking wine and *raki* (strong drink).

Garabed and Pertoosh joined in the fun, but when his friends jokingly offered Garabed wine, he refused. "Come on, Garabed, you're at a party!" A glass of wine was held to his lips. "Have some fun!"

"No!" Garabed drew back. To watch an abstainer stubbornly

28

refuse to partake of the drink they dearly loved seemed to infuriate his friends. All at once, several men seized him, throwing him to the floor. Two men sat on him while one tried to pour wine into his mouth. He was pinned to the floor, but to force his mouth open—that was something else!

They struggled to open his mouth, their fury increasing, but Garabed, equally adamant, kept his mouth sealed. Finally, failing in their efforts, they poured a full glass of wine over his mouth and face.

Toomas, watching the whole fiasco, thought they were not very smart, for they could have pinched his nose and forced him to open his mouth to breathe. But Toomas, of course, was not going to tell them!

Papa Garabed had only one fear. He lost his courage in deep water, for he had never learned to swim.

On one occasion he went partridge hunting with a group of men on the banks of the Euphrates River. Somehow, he became separated from his friends and could not find them. Seeing a bird in the air, he fired a shot and ran along the river to retrieve the fallen bird. Suddenly, his feet slipped and he fell into the river, which at that point was very deep and still.

Down, down, down he went with his heavy *shalvar* (wide trousers). He gasped and fought the water, struggling for his very life. There was no one around to rescue him, and he faced sure death.

Garabed's own words retell the rest of the story. "I felt some-one grab hold of my hair and pull me up. But my hair came off my head and I began to go down into oblivion once more. Then he, this 'someone,' reached down, grasped my neck with claw-like fingers, and like lightning, pulled me out of the water and threw me on the bank of the river.

"I don't know how long I remained there. When I regained consciousness, I looked around, amazed, but couldn't see or find anyone. The skin on my head was peeled off and my hair was gone. Yet I was not bleeding."

Garabed could never fully explain this mystery, except that he thought God had sent an angel to save his life.

Among the people who lived in Hini there was one who, it was believed, was demon-possessed. Khado, a poor old Kurdish peasant, wore a loose, shabby, dirty tunic over his bony shoulders and a raggedy wrap around his thin waist. Although baldheaded, he always wore a tattered turban and walked barefooted. He carried a stick for defensive purposes. It seemed he was always hungry, and he came often to Toomas's house to beg for food.

Khado had a deadly fear of cats. When Toomas and the children wanted to shoo him away, they would yell, "Khado, *pussing ama*! Khado, *pussing ama*!" ("Khado, the cat's going to get you!") Poor Khado would disappear like a streak of lightning, while the naughty boys laughed hysterically.

One day Khado saw Garabed and lunged upon him with all the fury of many demons. Garabed had to use all his strength to grab the peasant's arms with pincer-force and steer him into the house. Khado foamed at the mouth and fought with superhuman strength. Garabed shot orders, "We've got to get him into the yard. We've got to get the demons out of him." Turning to Pertoosh, he yelled, "Help me get him out into the yard." Then to Toomas he called, "Throw a quilt on the ground."

Toomas ran to do his father's bidding. Garabed and Pertoosh struggled with incredible might to drag poor Khado outside. Once in the yard, Garabed flung him to the ground and quickly rolled him up in the quilt right up to his neck. His arms became locked inside the quilt. He took another quilt and wrapped him again, then tied him spiral fashion with a rope, from his feet to his neck.

Now began Garabed's work of exorcism. He took the bundled and securely tied Khado and hanged him by his feet (with slack) from the beams under the veranda. Then he took a longer rope, tied one end of it to Khado's mid-region and wound the rest around his body. Taking the loose end, Garabed quickly ran from Khado, unwinding the rope as he went. Khado went spinning like a toy top. When the rope was completely unwound and Khado still spinning, Garabed ran back to him so that the rope would rewind around Khado's waist. Again Garabed ran from Khado, unwinding the rope as he went. To make sure the devils would come out, Garabed repeated the procedure three times.

After the breathless Khado had been unroped and released, he kept spinning on the ground, as if the spinning were still going on. When he stopped, he seemed stripped of all strength. His voice came out in a faint squeak.

Once recovered, Khado was never the same again. He seemed to be a liberated man, living in a new world, free of the demons who had possessed him. Garabed believed that he, as a Christian, had performed a work of mercy for Khado, a Moslem.

There had never been any doubt in Garabed's mind that devils do exist. He often told a story to the children of his own personal encounter with demons. Toomas's eyes would open wide as he listened to the chilling drama.

"At one time," Papa would say, "I was told that in a lone forsaken cobblestone cabin at the base of the mountain lived devils. One could not see them but they were there. Naturally, my curiosity was aroused." He smiled and twirled his moustache.

"And, of course, you had to go and find out," Pertoosh replied, also smiling. Everyone knew how much Garabed enjoyed a challenge or accepting a dare, another of his many traits of courage.

"Well, they gave me directions and I went to find this supposedly haunted cabin," he continued. "I had been warned before leaving not to take off my shoes while inside or put anything down on the floor, and to be sure to hold on to anything on my person.

"With such a challenge, I would do just the opposite. I left on my little journey with food, a dagger tucked in my sash around the waist, and a long cane in my hand.

"I opened the rickety door, which was unlocked, and walked cautiously inside, expecting anything at any moment. The room was empty—not even a bare bench to sit on—only a crude fireplace. One small window, a foot square, let in air and light.

"I leaned my cane on the wall next to the fireplace, took off my shoes, put them by the cane, and sat on the hearth on my folded legs.

"I had a big piece of *kesma* (food) in the fold of my sash. I took it out to eat. Suddenly, before it reached my mouth it was snatched out of my hand!

"Then things began to happen fast. My shoes started to walk on the floor with a great clatter. I got up, picked them up and sat on them."

At this point, Toomas would interrupt, his eyes wide open. "Papa, weren't you scared?"

"It all happened so fast I didn't have time to think," Garabed would reply. "I had some raisins and dried mulberries in my pocket. I felt a hand reach in my pocket, take them out and throw them on the floor.

"The cane that I had placed against the wall started to dance and jump up and down. Then it came and stood in front of me. I took my dagger out of its hilt and poked it all around the cane, thinking perhaps a hand was holding it."

Garabed reenacted the whole scene with dramatic gestures.

Then he continued, "All at once, it jumped and smacked me in the face. I grabbed it firmly but it broke in two. One piece remained in my hand. The other sailed through the open window.

"Then the shoes I was sitting on slipped away from under me. They began to knock me, first on one side of my face, then on the other.

"That did it! I took hold of my shoes and ran out as fast as I could. I never looked back. As I ran, I heard footsteps behind me. It sounded like a regiment of an army marching double-time, with heavy clatter. At the same time, millions of stones were being hurled at me. And all the while, I heard the horrible shouts and laughter."

At the end of the story, Pertoosh would ask, "Yes, and what did you learn from all this, my dear husband?"

A knowing smile would come over Garabed's face and he would say, "That devils *do* exist. They are real! Keep away from them!"

As Pertoosh sat and sewed on a cold winter evening, she reminisced, recalling many things about her husband, Garabed. In her thoughts, she could hear people calling, "Garabed, *aus urreh—on urreh—aus sheeneh—on sheeneh.*" ("Garabed, do this—do that—fix this—fix that.") Hini's chief fix-it man— that's what he was!

It pained her to remember how she sometimes had lost patience with him because he had never learned to say "no" to people and would let them take advantage of him. Dear, kind, conscientious Garabed. Perhaps she had been overbearing, but she hated to have anyone use and manipulate him.

Garabed, ever anxious to please her, would do anything not to incur her anger. For instance, there was the matter of giving the children their weekly baths, which was quite a ritual. "Garabed," Pertoosh would say, "don't forget the soap and the wood."

The family bath house was six blocks away. On his way there, Garabed would repeat, "Wood, children, soap; wood, children, soap; wood, children, soap," like a broken record. He must not, with so many things on his mind, forget what she wanted him to do.

In one corner of the bath house (situated directly under the Kurd's mosque) in the basement stood a stone slab with a small wooden stool over it where the bathers sat. Next to it, over an open fire, stood a boiler filled with water. Bathers carried the water in wooden buckets from the fountain nearby.

(The rest of the dark basement was a storage place for the lumber used by Garabed for making his exquisite hope chests, and for the crude lumber used for bridge building.)

As she continued her reminiscences, Pertoosh smiled when she recalled that, actually, she gave the most baths, not only to her own family, but to her sixty-odd nieces and nephews, even the married ones!

Each bather sat on a stool in front of her while she administered the scrubbing. When it involved her own children, after she had finished the scrubbing, Garabed would wrap each child in a large soft towel and one by one carry them home, making many trips back and forth.

In cold weather he had the pot-bellied stove going in the living room. Very gently he would deposit the child next to the stove, admonishing, "Be careful now. Don't get too close to the stove. See, it's red hot!" Occasionally, Toomas or Hovsep came too close to the red-hot stove with his bare buttocks and yelled, "Ouch," remembering too late the admonition.

And while Pertoosh reminisced about Garabed, she remembered how in his youth he had excelled in many sports, and how his friends had taken every opportunity to have fun with him because they knew of his fear of water. One day they had gone on a picnic by the river with a church group. They were having fun, when, without warning, several of his friends ran after him and threw him into the river.

For a moment Garabed seemed to panic. Seeing a tree nearby, he fastened his arms and legs around its trunk. His friends, laughing and joking, unfastened him and threw him once again into the water. Fortunately, Garabed discovered he was in shallow water and scrambled out safely.

Tree climbing had been one of his favorite sports. Everyone, both boys and girls, enjoyed this skill. The object was to climb as high as one could go without falling off.

On one occasion Garabed climbed a mulberry tree. While standing on a precarious branch eating the berries, he lost his footing and fell straight to the ground. As a result, he suffered an injured hip and from that time on walked with a slight limp. To add to this injury, rheumatism settled in the hip, sending him often to a local hot spring for relief, and on the one memorable occasion, all the way to Chermick.

Pertoosh remembered vividly the local spring, actually a mud-hole with its reddish-brown murky water. People said, "You can be cured of everything if you bathe yourself in the water.''

Near this pool stood a tree covered with rags of all colors, tied to its branches. The tree bore silent witness for every person who had bathed in the mudhole and had, supposedly, been cured. The cured individual would tear off a piece of his garment and tie it to the tree. The many faded, tattered rags were evidence that many generations had come here to bathe.

Even Dada Khazzar had come. But there were no rags to represent him and Garabed, because for them the spring had not effected a cure. ''Perhaps,'' they reasoned, ''because of the many years of usage, the water has lost its healing power.''

When it seemed certain that the local hot spring would not cure Garabed, Pertoosh had insisted that they try the waters of the famous hot springs at Chermick.

CHAPTER 10

The Approach of War

At Chermick, the Avedisians had hardly begun relaxing when the news of the war arrived. The impact of the terrible word came crashing in on Toomas's family, exploding all their plans, displacing their very souls.

Full of bewilderment, Toomas read the deep troubled concern that now lined his father's face. He studied the worried look in his mother's soft brown eyes. Mama had always like to sing, and on the journey her sweet voice had entertained them many times. Now no sweet songs came from her.

War, Toomas told himself, had to be something terrible to cause his parents to act as though the sun had stopped shining.

The family had gathered at the khan and stayed close together after the sad news came. Now Toomas, his voice full of apprehension, asked, ''Papa, what are we going to do now?''

Papa placed a large comforting hand on Toomas's shoulder. "We must get back to Hini at once." A look of urgency passed over his face. All at once a warm feeling came over Toomas. Yes! If they went home, then everything would be all right. Hini, their beloved home, would be a safe haven from that terrible thing called war. Papa and Mama would laugh again. They would all be safe and happy.

Mama broke in. "But Garabed, where shall we get the animals we need to take us back?" With the bellows of war, the hired escort with his horses, and all the people who owned animals, had fled.

Hovsep tried to be of help. "Papa, shall we go and try to find some animals to take us back?" The children knew that their parents' wealth could buy almost anything.

Papa's face brightened. "Yes, you and Toomas come with me." But try as they would, offering large sums of money for any kind of animal—horse, donkey or mule—none could be had for hire.

Two days passed. Though the spring sunshine promised to warm the bathers at Hot Springs, no one seemed to care to take advantage of it. Mama and Papa gathered the children around, opened the Bible, and read its promises. Mama reassured them, "We must trust God. Somehow we will be able to get home."

On the third day, word came that a caravan had formed to travel to Diyarbekir, a distance of three days' rapid travel.

"We will join the caravan," Papa said, smiling for the first time in several days. Ameh (Aunt) Toomig, one of his five sisters, lived in Diyarbekir. The news brought elation to everyone. "From Diyarbekir we will travel on to Hini," he added, trying to sound very assuring.

Their elation heightened when they were able to purchase a few donkeys for the trip. They joined the caravan and on the way met a steady unbroken chain of heavily loaded camels. Toomas and Hovsep tried to count them, but the chain faded from their line of vision like dots on a map.

Toomas's curiosity could not be contained. "Where are they going and what are they carrying?" he cried.

Hovsep, older and wiser, seemed to have the answer. "Papa says they are carrying arms and munitions." Then he explained the meanings of those words to Toomas.

The same questions disturbed the other members of the family. What did they carry? Where were they going? No one really knew.

Three days later the caravan arrived in Diyarbekir. Once they had arrived at Aunt Toomig's house, the family felt a sense of security.

That very night, their security vanished. Papa, awakened by the smell of smoke, ran through the house in his underwear, yelling, "Fire! Fire! Fire!"

A wild and uncontrolled fire had broken out over the city, filling the night with light like midday. The fire seemed to be concentrated over the entire Armenian business district.

Flames that seemed to be a mile high shot in every direction. No one had ever witnessed such a wild inferno. Panic struck every Armenian home. Women and children, some in shirts and chemises, some nude, fled from rooftop to rooftop, yelling and screaming. With roaring momentum, the conflagration swept through their stores and establishments, their sources of livelihood.

While the women kept the children close, comforting them and stilling their cries, the men went to try to help. They came from every direction, with buckets and five-gallon cans of water, coils of rope, long hooked poles, axes, shovels and picks. They were all running towards the sky-rocketing hot flames, but their desperate efforts were in vain—it was an impossible task, to put out those flames.

Men ran back and forth, trying to save a few valuables. Mothers, with their terrified children clinging to their skirts, ran helplessly, without direction. Some remained horrified and mute, watching all their earthly possessions vanish in the percolating flames.

The air was full of acrid, stinging smoke, which filled everyone's eyes and lungs. Toomas choked and cried, "Mama, I can't breathe." Pertoosh wet a cloth and placed it over his mouth and nose, directing everyone else to do the same.

The fire raged and burned through the night, into the dawn, and all the next day and night. It consumed with raging vengeance every last vestige of everything owned by the Armenian people in the business district of the city.

At last, nothing remained but charred stone walls. Chimneys stood grotesquely above smoke-oozing ashes. The entire business district of the city, well-known for its black porous stones, lay in piles and piles of half-burned rubbish. Tumbled heaps of black stones clogged the streets, and for days horrible, choking smoke permeated the air.

Crowds of people pried the hot smoldering ashes, trying desperately to salvage anything they could. What they could not know was that this terrible fire was only the beginning of the ravages that war would bring to them.

And now the people who had lost their every means of livelihood asked themselves how this terrible thing had come about. To wipe out an entire business district so thoroughly would have been impossible had it not been planned. Everyone knew the answer. The Turks, hearing that war had been declared, had gone to work to perform their own evil deeds against the Armenians— burn their businesses, destroy their means of livelihood, then what could they do?

The enemy, sinister and as yet unseen, had begun its diabolical work against the Christians.

What next? No one knew. Gaunt, haunted eyes told the story of sadness, heartache and despair. What would they do now?

Toomas, having witnessed the inferno, at last comprehended fully the meaning of *war*. It meant people full of hatred, bent on destroying those they hated.

After remaining in the city a few more days to comfort and help those who had lost all their possessions, Papa said they should be moving on to Hini. He reasoned, "There we will be among the Kurds with whom our people have lived for centuries. They are not like the Turks in this city. We know how to deal with them." His voice held such assurance that it brought comfort to his family.

How could Garabed know otherwise?

Papa hired a number of horses and mules and a warrior muleteer to protect them from possible attacks on their two-day journey to Hini. Once home, he said, they would be safe. Hini, geographically isolated, could not possibly become enmeshed in war. Home meant peace and safety.

The Kurds who lived in Hini were not like the Turks. The Avedisian family had always had a good rapport with them. Four thousand Kurds lived in Hini on one end, and four thousand Armenians lived on the other end. They had lived together for generations. True, there had been uprisings sometimes, but the Armenians had always been in control. The Kurds in Hini needed the Armenian skills and finances. They could not exist without them.

In 1895, the Turkish government under the reign of Abdul Hamid II had waged war against the Armenians. He had earned the names of "Abdul, the Bloody" and "Great Assassin," because of the massacre of Armenians under his rule. But that was all in the past; surely that would never happen again.

CHAPTER 11

Journey to Hini

The family said goodbye to Aunt Toomig and started on the last two days of their interrupted journey home. Everyone was anxious to get back to Hini.

On the evening of the first day they came to a lush carpet of green beside a creek, and Papa announced, "We will stay here for the night." The spring sunshine had warmed them as they traveled, but it had been a long, weary day, and Pertoosh was glad it was time to stop. They alighted from their animals and began to make camp as the sun's fiery rays splashed bright color across the sky.

All at once, Toomas, ever observing, ever alert, spotted a band of soldiers in the distance, coming their way. "Mama, Papa, look! There are soldiers coming toward us!" he cried excitedly. Never had he seen so many men marching.

Instantly, Garabed shaded his eyes and turned to gaze into the distance. At the same time, Pertoosh instinctively murmured a prayer, while Aunt Nunia pulled little Loosig close. Soldiers? What could it mean? As they drew near, it could be seen that they were Kurdish soldiers in uniform. "Of course," Pertoosh told herself, "they are marching off to war."

To everyone's surprise, looking as though he would drop from exhaustion any moment, the family's servant Kootig appeared among the marching troops.

Pertoosh felt the uneven rhythm of her heart. They had left Kootig, their faithful servant of many years, at home to look after things. What could he be doing among the Kurds? Her eyes met Garabed's and she saw the shocked look upon his face.

The soldiers came closer, and now they saw Kootig's face clearly. Always healthy and vibrant, now he presented a pathetic picture, clothed in rags and shriveled up like a prune. What had happened to him? Toomas, who had nicknamed him Kootig (small box), did not even recognize him.

Now the soldiers came close to the camp and marched right past it. As Kootig marched by, Garabed called to him. He turned, and when he saw the man he had served faithfully for so many years, his eyes filled with crushing sorrow. They seemed to say, "Why did you allow *them* to do this to me?" He stepped out of the line and came to the camp.

Trying to grasp the situation, Pertoosh and Garabed expressed their shock and compassion to their servant. Kootig looked as though he were already wasting away from starvation. Pertoosh quickly fetched him some bread and cheese, which he snatched from her, and, cupping a hand under his chin (a habit he had had for years), he ate like a starving man. Not until Toomas saw that familiar gesture did he "see" Kootig.

After he had eaten, Kootig told the incredible story. After war had been declared, the Kurdish soldiers of Hini had gone to every Armenian home and said, "If you wish to keep the war away from your families, if you wish to protect them, all Armenian men must enlist with the Turkish Army and come with us to serve our government."

The Armenian men had protested, "But we are not Kurds nor Turks. We are Armenians."

"No matter," they had replied. "The Turkish government has promised to give protection to your families if you will enlist and give assistance to us."

At last they persuaded the Armenian fathers, sons and brothers, each of whom would do anything to protect his family, to enlist in the Turkish Army. And since Kootig's blood ran Armenian, he too felt compelled to join.

After being recruited, the men began to march. The Armenian men were not given clothing appropriate for army duty but wore clothing that soon turned to rags. They were not told where they were going or when they would arrive. (Later it would turn out that they would be used to build roads and do the heaviest kind of construction work.)

Kootig related how they had marched day in and day out without food. As the soldiers marched past the family's camp, the Armenian men were easy to spot. They wore rags, and the pangs of hunger had etched the picture of starvation on their faces.

Garabed and Pertoosh called boldly to as many as they could to come into their camp. Pertoosh, her heart aching, gave food and drink to all of them. Each told the story that Kootig had told. Pertoosh wished she could erase the sorrowful looks on their faces, caused by having to leave their families so suddenly and not knowing where they were going or whether they would ever see their loved ones again.

In her heart she offered a silent prayer. Had they been in Hini, Garabed, her beloved, would have been taken. He had been spared, at least for the time being—but who knew what awaited them?

The children had gathered around the men. Pertoosh saw the anger and resentment on her young son's face and knew that Toomas's comprehension of the meaning of the word *war* was increasing.

That night the family shared their bedding with these men. The next day, after the men had left to catch up with the other soldiers, the Avedisian family broke camp. All day, as they traveled, they encountered hundreds, thousands, of Kurdish soldiers. On their feet they wore the *jaruks* of war (laced sandals worn by the infantry).

Toomas, always close to Hovsep, stared in wonderment. "Millions of them," he said aloud. Hovsep nodded.

Each time the soldiers walked past them, Garabed and the warrior escort placed themselves between the family and the soldiers. "Dear Garabed," Pertoosh told herself. "He will protect us with his very life, if necessary."

As the thousands of soldiers marched past them Pertoosh saw the fear mounting on Toomas's face. Everyone had heard the story of the Kurdish soldiers. People said they were like a swarm of grasshoppers. Wherever they lighted the greenery disappeared.

Again Pertoosh murmured a silent prayer in her heart, for not being molested by the soldiers.

As they neared their beloved Hini, the children began to show their excitement and Pertoosh noticed that Garabed's face had lost its worried look. Aunt Nunia appeared to be her happy self and the children were more playful than they had been.

At last Toomas spied the rooftops. "Look," he cried, pointing a finger in the distance. "Mama, Papa, everybody! We are home!"

CHAPTER 12

Hini, Unprepared for War

As the sun vanished into the horizon, the family entered its beloved Hini. Had it been months since they had left it, instead of weeks?

Toomas wanted to run, but Pertoosh held him back. "But, Mama, I can't wait to see 'Oolo' (his favorite name for his sister Victoria). I want to see my cousins, too." He referred to Victoria's two little sons.

Pertoosh felt the same excitement and smiled. Yet, as the family walked slowly through the cobblestone streets, things did not seem the same. Something sinister and frightening seemed to hover over the whole village. There was no one in the streets. Where were the people? No one ran to greet them, and the usual hubbub of activity was missing.

Garabed led his little caravan through the streets that had no names and past the houses that had no numbers.

The sun had set and darkness came swiftly. Pertoosh lit the kerosene lamps. When the boys returned from helping Garabed, she said it was time for bed. They had already notified the relatives of their return. Reluctantly, the boys drew their sleeping mats from the pile in the living room and threw them on the floor.

Pertoosh noticed the troubled look on Toomas's face. She knelt beside the boys. The children never went to sleep without saying their prayers, nor would they go to sleep until she rubbed their backs and sang a lullaby. Now she crooned, "Sweet children, nice children, fold your arms and close your big eyes, and when you wake up, be like Jesus." A serenity came over the children and soon they were asleep. A look of trust had come over Toomas's face, and Pertoosh was satisfied.

While the children slept, Pertoosh and Garabed discussed the horrors of the past few days. Pertoosh had not wanted to reveal her fears before the boys. Now she asked, "Garabed, why are the Kurds doing this to our people?" Her soft brown eyes were filled with the hurt in her heart.

While they talked, Dada Khazzar and Sopig Mama entered the room. After welcoming their son and Pertoosh, they fell into a strange silence. "What is it, Papa?" Garabed asked. "We saw hundreds, yes, thousands of our men marching to war. How could this happen in such a short time?" Dada Khazzar blew his nose. "The Kurds came for our men. And the Chachans are here, too." Bending his gray head, he placed his hands over his face, avoiding their glances. Another cold chill squeezed Pertoosh's heart. No words came.

"The Chachans? Here in Hini?" Garabed echoed. A flush of red colored his face and his eyes blazed at the outrageous thought.

"Yes, they're in the mountains, all around us," Sopig Mama cried, terror choking her voice.

Pertoosh's vocal cords remained frozen. The very word "Chachan" struck terror into every Armenian heart. Known for their unparalleled diabolical deeds, they were a beastlike tribe. They ate and slept with their animals in one-room subterranean huts. Instead of toiling, tilling, and harvesting like the local Kurds, this wild, rude and barbarous tribe of mountaineers hid in forests and caves and preyed on wealthy travelers. They were descendants of the ancient Parthians, who were well known as a semi-savage race. Their presence in these parts spelled the worst kind of trouble.

"Why did our men go?" Garabed persisted.

"The Kurds promised safety to our families. They said war would not come to our homes if they went to fight for the government." Dada Khazzar spoke with a defeated tone.

"Do you believe them?" Garabed asked.

"No. But I don't know what to believe."

Pertoosh's voice returned at last. "Which ones of our men did they take?"

Dada Khazzar's eyes filled with sadness. "Mostly the young men of Hini."

"Did Hovaness and Krikor have to go?" Garabed asked.

"Not yet." Dada Khazzar placed his arm around Sopig Mama, who had begun to shake. "Come, my dear," he said softly. "Let's go to bed and let the children rest." Sopig Mama nodded and they walked toward the door.

That night sleep did not come to Pertoosh. Long before the sun came up, while it was still dark, she had jumped from her mat to face the new day. Garabed, who had also twisted and turned all night, flung aside his blanket and followed her.

They moved about quietly in order not to awaken the exhausted children. While Pertoosh combed her long flowing hair and piled it on top of her head, she spoke in a low tone, "Garabed, do you think the Kurds and Chachans will allow the Armenians to continue to work in their stores and shops now?"

Garabed, already dressed and buttoning his shirt, replied, "Who knows what those half-human Chachans will do?" In the dim light of the kerosene lamp Pertoosh saw his features darken.

"But the Kurds need us. They know how valuable we Armenians are to them. Your brother Hovaness is an expert at building bridges and houses. And Krikor—no one is more skilled in making wooden buckets and wooden plows than he. Your brothers are master craftsmen!"

"Yes, that's more than we can say for the Kurds. They depend on us for everything," Garabed had to admit.

"Surely the Kurds will let them stay and work at their trades," Pertoosh's voice rose. "And surely our friend, Musso, will not turn against us. Why, you and your brothers built his beautiful home."

"Yes, he's pretty wealthy and influential. I hope he will not turn against us," Garabed replied. "He's always been our friend."

"And what about you, Garabed? Will they allow you to work in your shop?"

Garabed, a master marquetry craftsman, had always been in demand by the Kurds. They loved the work of his hands, every item finished with infinite perfection. An expert at producing beautiful backgammon boards, he delighted the Kurds, who purchased every one he made. Every inch of the boards—inside, outside, over, under—revealed his precision and expertise. The tables and legs, inlaid without nails, with gems of wood, ivory, metal and polished stones of different colors, were works of art.

"Perhaps they will allow me to stay as Hini's fix-it man," Garabed said. But Pertoosh saw the faint smile of sarcasm. As the man who made minor repairs for everyone in Hini, mending fences or leaky wooden buckets, replacing broken shovels or spade handles, renovating broken violins and even making new ones, he and his services were very much in demand by Kurds and Armenians alike.

Equally in demand were the hope chests Garabed made from the finest hardwood brought down from Mt. Ararat (where Noah's Ark was supposed to have landed).

Pertoosh remembered Victoria's young husband. "Did they take him, too? Oh, we must find out." She glanced out the window and saw a faint tinge of the sun.

"Soon it will be daylight," Garabed said. "We will go to see them." Victoria and her husband lived with their children in another section of Hini.

While they talked the sun came up and lighted the sky. Later in the morning they visited Victoria and found her husband still at home. As they ventured about the village to see what was going on, they could not believe their eyes. Gone from the faces of the Armenians was the look of peace and tranquility which had so accurately reflected their contentment. People darted furtively and fearfully in and out of their homes. Rumors about the fate of the Armenians spread like a raging river.

Soon it became apparent that the lives of the men who thought that by escaping they would be safe with their families, were not safe at all. The Kurds, with whom they had lived for centuries, who had at times shared their festivities, now became the enemy at war—open war—with the *giaours*. The cross of Christendom stood between the Turkish Moslems and the Armenian Christians.

In the days that followed the Kurds began their systematic

work—to seek out and imprison all the Armenian men in Hini. No one, young, middle-aged or old, would be spared.

Victoria's young husband became one of the first to be imprisoned. Coming to Pertoosh and Garabed with her two chubby little boys, she sobbed, "They have taken him away. Oh, Mama, what will they do to him?"

Pertoosh's heart cried with her daughter. Placing her arms around Victoria's sobbing body, she tried to console her.

Toomas, standing nearby, could not bear to see his sister cry as though her heart would break. He loved his Oolo. "Don't cry, Oolo," he said. "Mama will pray and he will be all right." He placed his little hand on her hair in a tender caress.

A knock at the door brought Aunt Khanum and Aunt Shooshan, each holding a small child by the hand. Their faces showed the fear that filled their hearts. Victoria wiped her tears. Pertoosh greeted her sisters-in-law, then turned to Toomas and said, "Take the little ones, Toomas, and go play on the roof." She kissed them and gave them a handful of raisins. "Where is Hovsep? He can play with you, too."

"Hovsep is at the shop with Papa making *knolleens* (wooden shoes)." Every Armenian boy received training in skills and trades, and Hovsep had become an expert at making wooden shoes.

"Then take Looderr and Aram and play, but watch them carefully."

Toomas took his four-year-old cousin Looderr and five-year-old cousin Aram by the hand and headed for the rooftop, calling back, "All right, Mama, I'll watch them."

The Horrors of Jail

In the days that followed, although birds warbled their songs of spring, for the Armenians the sun had ceased to shine. With systematic precision, the Kurds and Chachans went from door to door, with no warning, intent upon flushing out every Armenian male.

Early one morning Toomas was visiting a cousin and playing on the porch with the children. The main door had been locked, and they were gleefully going in and out of the house through an open window. Suddenly three huge Kurdish soldiers, armed with guns and khandjars, brushed past the children and went to the door. They turned the knob and when the door failed to open, they began to pound, uttering loud curses.

One soldier, eyes blazing, yelled, "Open the door!" Inside, the frightened occupants pretended not to hear. Toomas watched in horror as the soldiers battered the door, which was two inches thick, made of solid walnut.

The door would not yield to their blows. With more loud curses, they took their axes, and with the fury of many demons they shattered the door to pieces. It took ten minutes, and their rage accelerated with each passing moment.

Toomas felt the wild gallop of his heart. What did the soldiers want? Why were they so full of anger? And why hadn't they seen the open window? They must be terribly stupid, he told himself.

He watched with increasing terror as they entered, seized the young husband with their grip of iron, and held him fast.

"You will come with us," thundered the leader, his voice full of contempt.

The young man struggled to free himself, but to no avail. "Where to? Where to?" he gasped.

The soldier would not tell him that jail was his destination. "You will join the Turkish army and fight for the government."

"But I am an Armenian, not a Turk." The youth made another

attempt to free himself, only to meet with a strong blow to his face.

"You will join the army and help us keep the war from coming to Hini. If you join us, your family will be safe."

"Do you mean no harm will ever come to my family if I go with you and join the army?" The Kurd had used the one persuasive argument that reached the heart of every Armenian male. The family was the very reason for his existence. He would do anything, even yield his life, to protect his family.

"Yes," boomed the leader; then with an evil smile, "Otherwise, they will die." They yanked the young man toward the door.

"Wait!" screamed his wife. "You cannot take him this way. Let me get his shoes, shirt and coat."

Her words fell on deaf ears.

"Please, please, let me say goodbye to my husband," she begged, tears bathing her face.

"Let me say goodbye to my wife," the young husband entreated, as he struggled with all his might to wrench himself away.

One soldier struck another blow across his face and dragged him out of the house, leaving behind his hysterical wife.

Toomas could not believe what he had seen. The actions of these men filled him with shock and terror. They would not give a moment of time for the Armenian men to plant a farewell kiss, give their wives a parting caress, bend over the cradles of their sleeping babies, or even say a prayer before parting.

Toomas did not know that this parting he had witnessed, and those of all the other men, would be for forever, on this earth.

Not wasting a moment, he ran home to tell his parents what had happened. Mama listened and her sorrow filled her soft eyes.

"Will the soldiers come and take Papa?" Toomas cried.

Pertoosh placed a finger over his mouth. "Hush, my little one," she said.

"But, Mama," Toomas persisted, "those soldiers came and took my cousin away. He'll never come back. I *know* he won't." Toomas could not hold the tears back.

"Come, Toomas," Mama whispered. "Let us boil some eggs for Easter." She mustered a smile. "Yes, this coming Sunday is Easter." And for a moment, Toomas forgot the terrible scene he had witnessed. Easter was a day which was always approached with excitement and anticipation, although when it came that year, fear and apprehension had filled the heart of every Armenian family and the usual joy and games were missing.

As the Kurds and Chachans continued their work of invasion and the incarceration of Armenian men, some of the men, to evade the captors, disguised themselves in women's garments and hid in underground passages and cellars, sharing the animals' living quarters. Outnumbered as they were, they did not dare offer open resistance.

To make matters worse, the Kurds and Chachans, by order of the government, now went about searching for and confiscating all weapons owned by the giaours. Every Armenian family possessed as many weapons as the government would allow. Now their weapons were to be taken away, leaving them without protection. The men in prison were warned, "Unless your families surrender their weapons, they will die."

In jail was the minister of the village, a shrewd leader. When the Kurdish guards grilled the jailed men without mercy, compelling them to confess to the possession of weapons in their homes, he advised, "No! Do not surrender your ammunition. If you do, we will all be lost. Our families will die. Ammunition is power!"

But the men were wishful thinkers and gullible. Eager to believe that their families would be spared if they surrendered their arms, most of them agreed to comply. "You *will* spare our families if we surrender our weapons?" they pleaded.

"Spare your families? But of course!" answered the Kurds.

While the minister continued to counsel his parishioners against the folly of surrendering their arms, the men preferred to believe the Kurds. What they did not know was that they actually had no alternative.

In the days that followed, whether or not the men agreed (a few dissented), they were dragged from jail to their homes. Under threat of death they were compelled to surrender their weapons. They were forced to go from house to house with picks and shovels to dig the grounds for hidden arms. With a dozen rifles thrust at their backs, they were persuaded to "*dig!*" Inside the houses axes were put to work.

Rather than surrender their arms to the Kurds, families had already begun to hide them in walls, wells, staircases, floors, cellars, or anyplace that could be excavated.

The Kurds came daily, sometimes hourly, to ransack homes, to confiscate firearms, and to search for concealed men. They knew the Armenian men very well, and had an accurate count of those in jail and those still at large.

Garabed, as yet, had not been apprehended. Knowing that the Kurds would soon come for all the men in the Avedisian household, he said, "Before they come for us, we will destroy all our documents and records."

"Why, Papa?" Toomas wanted to know.

"Because if they find anything about our Christian history, it will be held against us. In fact, all of our records will be held against us."

Toomas and Hovsep went to work with their parents. Mama brought out all the documents that contained references to Armenian Christianity, churches, schools or any educational society. The fireplace burned brightly as statistics, atlases, Armenian textbooks, Armenian history books, Armenian novels, went up in smoke.

As the flames shot upward, Toomas observed the sadness on his parents' faces. Papa's face showed the sorrow in his heart. Mama's brown eyes, misty with tears, touched his own heart. What would they do now? Mama said over and over, "We are in God's hands."

After all the documents had become ashes, only one precious book remained. The large family Bible, which contained the Avedisian family record, must at all costs be preserved. "Where shall we hide it? The Kurds must not find it!" Pertoosh said with a sorrowful voice.

"Yes," agreed Garabed. "It's been in our family for generations. It's our only remaining record. They must not find it!"

He looked around the house for a good hiding place. In the meantime, Mama had dropped on her knees and prayed, "Lord God, our refuge and our strength. We pray that your Word, your precious Word may be preserved from our enemies. We pray that this Bible may be preserved, that our children may possess it always."

Hearing Mama's prayer, Toomas again felt confidence. *Nothing* was going to happen to their precious Bible that Mama and Papa read from every day.

At last Papa found a place. "We will hide it in the wall," he said, with a pleased look. "They will not find it." Removing a board from the living room wall, they placed the large Bible, which Pertoosh had carefully wrapped, behind the board. Garabed then replaced the board so skillfully that no one would guess it had ever been removed.

"They will have to remove the wall board by board to find it," Garabed said, with finality in his voice.

Last Goodbyes

Pertoosh awoke one morning with the feeling that this would be the day Garabed, her beloved, would be snatched from his family and taken to jail. Her heart ached with heavy gloom.

Garabed had already prepared his family. With a forced smile he told the children, "I do not know how long they will keep us prisoners. Perhaps the war will not last long. If they compel us to fight in the Turkish army we will have to do so." He placed his arms around Toomas and Hovsep. "Boys, be good and always remember the adz and the saw," Garabed admonished.

Toomas never forgot his father's oft-repeated Christian ethic: Don't be an adz, to always take (pull toward you); but be a saw, to give and take.

"You will be the men of the family when I am gone," he continued, his eyes filled with pity for his two young sons.

"Yes, Papa. Hovsep and I will take care of Mama." Toomas began to cry, clinging to his father's neck.

Papa held him close. "But God will be with you. Take good care of Mama." His eyes were brimmed with tears.

Hovsep, brushing the tears from his own eyes, said, "Don't worry, Papa. I'm old enough to take care of Mama and the animals and the house."

Garabed loosened his hold and turned to Pertoosh. "You see, my dear, you have two young men to look after you and the house until I return."

Pertoosh mustered a smile to cover Garabed's words. She felt in her heart that once he was taken away he would not return. She turned her face so Garabed would not see the ache that stabbed her very soul.

Her intuition proved correct, for scarcely had she finished making breakfast for the family when there came the dreaded pounding on the door. Garabed, who had sat down to eat, jumped to his feet, grabbed Toomas and Hovsep, kissed them soundly, then turned to Pertoosh and embraced her, as though he could not let her go.

The Kurds at the door twisted the knob. When it failed to open, they gave a loud oath and resumed their pounding. Garabed kissed his wife, whispering, "We will meet again. God will take care of you."

"Yes, my dear husband, do not worry. God will take care of us."

Garabed released his hold on Pertoosh. "Let me open the door before they break it down."

The Kurds entered, fully armed. Again they made their one-way proposition, "If you will come with us, join the Turkish army and fight for Turkey, your family will be protected."

"You will be sure to protect my family?" Garabed asked.

"Oh, but of course. No harm will come to them, if you come with us."

With one last clinging look, Garabed was led away, with Toomas crying, "No, no, no. Don't take my papa away!"

The door closed. The click, for Pertoosh, ended a long, beautiful chapter in her life.

They watched from the window as the Avedisian men—uncles, nephews, brothers—were all snatched and dragged away to jail. Now, Pertoosh told herself, all the women were alone. With their men in jail, the women were like ships without rudders, lost at sea, at the mercy of the Christian-hating Mohammedans. As the days of spring sped by, the women retreated to themselves. They congregated, tried to console one another, and prayed incessantly.

The men in hiding did not remain there long. The Kurds and Chachans persisted in their search daily. Knowing which ones were missing, they went to their homes, and grilled the wives and children without mercy. At last, these Armenian husbands and fathers, unable to endure the knowledge that their loved ones were being tortured, surrendered one by one to their suppressors. With cruel vengeance they were flung into jail.

The Kurds did not provide food for their prisoners and the women were not allowed to visit, but the children were permitted to bring food.

One morning Pertoosh packed a basket of food for Garabed with his favorites, pilaff, dried mulberries fried with eggs, ka-woor-ma, and a handful of raisins and nuts. Handing the basket to Toomas, she said, "Tell him—we are praying for the men—"

Her voice choked up with emotion. "Go quickly and be careful."

"Yes, Mama. Don't worry." Toomas had seen the tears that welled in her eyes.

When Toomas and his cousins, Arsen and Dickran, arrived at the jail with their baskets of food, they were stopped by a guard who snatched the baskets and searched them. He helped himself to a handful of raisins and nuts from each basket before he returned the baskets and let the boys enter.

Through the dim light, the boys saw them—fathers, uncles, brothers and sons—all on their knees in a circle with the minister in the center. Unashamed of the tears in their eyes, they prayed softly, "Father, give us courage to be faithful. Take care of our families. Thy will be done."

All at once the men spotted the boys. Instantly Garabed was on his feet, grabbing Toomas. Arsen and Dickran were snatched by

52

their father, Krikor. Garabed held Toomas close. Toomas felt his heart beat as his father crushed him against his manly breast, showering breathless burning kisses on his face, his eyes, his cheeks, his lips, crying, "Toomas, my son, my son!"

Toomas gazed into his father's feverish eyes, submerging his soul into their depth. He devoured the high forehead, the fine dominant nose, the twirling moustache he loved so much. "Papa, Papa, Papa!" he cried.

In that moment of communion Toomas felt the floodgates open and his father's love and blessings fill his heart. Father and son were united in a bond of affection—a moment sublime—a moment that would be treasured forever.

The other men likewise grabbed the boys and smothered them avidly with hot kisses and hugs.

Within a few moments, the guard returned and with a rough arm snatched the boys from their fathers and led them out the door.

Two days later, when the children again took food to their fathers in jail, they saw that the evil process of execution had already begun.

With diabolical fervor, the Kurds inflicted the pre-death atrocities. These included pulling out moustaches, beards and fingernails with pliers, cutting off tongues and ears, plucking eyes out of their sockets, applying red-hot tongs, brass plates or horseshoes to the most tender parts of the body, partially or completely emasculating the men, and inflicting other disfigurations.

Some men were thrown into wells, then removed and tied to the tails of donkeys or mules and dragged along the cobblestone streets while being lashed with deadly whips.

Others were taken to the homes of prominent Kurds and butchered around the fountains in the courtyards as sacrificial offerings.

Many of the men offered all their possessions to their executioners, pleading, "You may have our money, our jewels, all our possessions, if you will shoot us quickly."

With demonic glee, the Kurds replied, "A Christian's life is not worth the price of a bullet!"

To add to the horror, these Mohammedans encouraged their own children to take part in the work of torturing and exterminating the giaours. Kurdish fathers stood by and watched with ancestral pride while their children carried out in cold blood the deliberate slaughter of defenseless men.

CHAPTER 15

No Tears for Toomas

Among the young men who were sacrificed to the khandjars that night was Garabed's nephew, Meeron. As Meeron was being led away, Garabed, wanting to give him courage and to reaffirm their faith, said in Armenian, "Meeron, *me vaghnar, katch egheer! Or mu ergink beedee hantibink.*" ("Meeron, don't be afraid. Be brave! We will meet each other in heaven.")

The Kurds, not understanding the language, deduced that some conspiracy existed between the two. Leaving Meeron temporarily, they took Garabed instead. Out in the courtyard, they lashed and kicked him with heavy boots until his life had almost ebbed away. Then they dragged his body inside, over the steps.

No one ever knew how many crushed bones and internal injuries Garabed received in return for his fatherly, sympathetic words to his nephew.

That day, May 14, would be indelibly branded in Toomas's memory, for he saw his father shortly after the terrible beating. He found him prostrate and motionless on the floor. Ugly welts had risen where the lashes had fallen. Deep discolorations all over his body bore the imprints of the Kurds' boots. Swollen bruises bore testimony to his having been dragged on the ground and stairway.

Toomas knelt in horror beside his father, beside the good kind father who did not even know how to hurt another's feelings! What had they done to him? A violent feeling of revenge welled up within Toomas. He wanted, with all the strength of his young body, to pay them back for what they had done to his father.

"Papa, Papa, Papa!" he cried. "What did they do to you?" Had his father died? he wondered.

Garabed, hearing his son's voice, opened his eyes slowly. Toomas heard low, suppressed groans. He guessed that although externally his father withheld acknowledgment of his pain, inside he was writhing in agony. Toomas knew at that moment that the memory of his father in this condition would haunt him as long as he lived.

He wanted to scream in protest, but he stifled a cry, lest the guard hear him. Inside his heart, he cried to God for revenge, "God, why are you letting them do this? God, strike them dead for what they did to my father!"

Toomas would always remember his father and the other brave Armenian men who had feared nothing, even death itself. These men had not died in battle, with a chance to defend themselves, but had been defenseless while their lives were extracted from them. He would always remember that these men had died for their faith. Not once did Toomas see a sign that these Christian warriors had wavered in favor of Mohammedanism. Christianity had been ingrained within their very souls.

While Toomas's hot tears spilled on Garabed's swollen face, Garabed tried to show some sign of life. Toomas saw his efforts, each breath bringing agony and pain. He heard the words, a faint whisper, "Toomas—my—son. You must not think—of revenge. Trust in God. These men—do—not—know—God. They are— under—the influence of—Satan."

Papa had read his thoughts. He could *not* understand why Papa did not want revenge, but to satisfy his father, he nodded his head.

When he went home and told Pertoosh what had happened, her eyes filled with profound agony. She went into the other room, and though Toomas knew his mother feared nothing, he heard her cries, her tears of sorrow for what they had done to her beloved husband.

She returned with dry eyes and spoke in a low composed tone, "Go, Toomas, take this mat to your father. Perhaps it will give him a little comfort."

Gladly, Toomas took the mat and ran to the jail, but the guard at the door snatched it from him and retained it for his own comfort. A rage of rebellion stirred within Toomas, yet he could not say a word. The guard laughed and said, "Your father will not need this mat."

What did he mean? Toomas turned and ran, crying tears of outrage all the way home. "God," he pleaded, "strike them dead!"

Upon his return to the jail the next morning, Toomas learned what the guard had meant. His father was dead! They had finished him off with their horrible khandjars earlier that morning.

Toomas could not control his wild feelings. He ran past the guard, who only snarled and laughed at him. He called to God, "Why, oh why, did you let them do this to my papa? Why, God? Do you hear me? Why? Why? My father was a good man!"

Inside his heart—lest God hear him—he vowed that someday his father's death would be avenged.

How could he go home and tell Mama? How could he and the other children tell their mothers that not only had Garabed fallen victim to the khandjars, but that all the Avedisian prisoners were dead.

The guards had made no attempt to hide the remains of those whom they had massacred. How could these children describe the details, the final horrible account of how the men had died? Toomas thought, "If I were only older, just for one day!"

After they left the prison, he and the other children walked the streets of Hini, strangely silent—children without laughter, children without fathers, children now in cold shock.

At home they found the women sitting on the floor along the wall, crying. How could they bring them even more mournful news? How could they add fresh fuel to the already blazing pyre?

When Pertoosh saw the boys as they walked into the room, an expression came over her face as though an arrow had pierced her heart. "Papa—Papa is—Papa is dead!" Toomas blurted out. But Pertoosh knew already.

Now all the women burst into a frenzy of wailing. Had the roof on the house not been as strong as it was, the intensity of their cries, raging and storming, would have blown it off, supports, rafters, beams and all.

Everyone, even the very youngest two-year-old cousins, sat shedding torrents of tears. Pertoosh wailed inconsolably. Like Rachel in the Bible, she "would not be comforted." She had gone far beyond the bounds of comfort.

Hovsep broke into sobs. Dada Khazzar (who had not yet been imprisoned) and Sopig Mama heard the wails and came rushing into the house. Ameh Shooshan screamed and fainted.

As he watched everyone's tears flowing so profusely, Toomas found that, while yesterday he cried bitterly for his father's agony, today his tear ducts refused to flow. They had completely dried out. Try as he might, he could not shed a single tear.

And oh, how he wanted to cry. How could he, Garabed's son, watch even his little cousins sob, while he sat dry-eyed? He knew that he should cry, at least to show the others that he, too, felt the sorrow they were feeling. Turning his face toward the wall, he rubbed his eyes, trying to force his eye muscles and tear ducts to spill tears. Nothing happened. Oh, why couldn't he cry?

Was it because of his intense love for his father, or his deep hatred for his slayers? Or was it because the things he had seen at the jail had severed the threads of his emotions and he could no longer feel or cry?

While he rationalized, the thought persisted: If he did not cry, later people would say, "When Toomas's father died, the boy never shed a tear."

> *Whispered the mute language of sorrow:*
> *"Toomas dear, your father's dead!*
> *But no sob, no tear—a heart of lead?"*

"But my father did not die! He was beaten and butchered, murdered! There's a difference between dying naturally and being slaughtered bit by bit!"

Nevertheless, he had to show his mother, his sister, his brother, all his relatives and everyone, that his heart was not encased in lead. Since the tears would not flow naturally, he would resort to simulated tears.

Going outside, he spat in the palm of his hand and moistened his eyes with his saliva. Then he came inside and showed himself. There! That was better. This should keep tongues from wagging in the future.

No one, however, noticed his childish efforts, not even Pertoosh. Pierced by the anguish in her heart, blinded by the tears in her eyes, she saw no one.

The massacre continued until all the Armenian men of Hini, except a handful, had been wiped out. Without husbands and fathers, the women and children remained indoors, for the most part. What was going to happen to them? No one knew yet. Huddled together, they mourned and prayed.

CHAPTER 16

The Shambles

Pertoosh longed for word from her son in America, but since the massacre had started, no mail had reached her. And there was no way for him to know that his father had been massacred for his Christian faith. In her prayers Pertoosh often said, "Lord, we thank you for leading our son Aghegsanter to America. Would that we had all gone!"

A short time after Garabed's death, a report of new horror reached Pertoosh. Amo Krikor, who still made tools for the Kurds, brought the news. The extermination of every Armenian man had only been the beginning. The plan of extermination went much further. The massacre was to continue until every man, woman and child had been destroyed. The order had gone throughout the land that every Armenian must perish.

Already Armenians from other villages and cities had been seized by surprise from their homes and herded in groups to form a death march. Without food and water or appropriate clothing or footwear, they had been led away—not to the khandjar, but to march, in intense heat and bitter cold, for hundreds of miles. Their destination? Those who did not die enroute from hunger, thirst, exposure or exhaustion would reach the great desolate desert, to die there.

In Hini the Kurds continued their reign of terror. Beginning at the borders of the village, they worked their way toward the center of the village. At first they took their victims to the slaughter a few at a time. As they became more experienced, they took a large number of the women and children and held them in a detention building.

The Protestant church, located conveniently at the suburb of the village, was converted into what the Armenians now called *tuchoghkee doon* (hell-house). From this building, which was packed most of the time, they were taken a short distance away to the "shambles" where the slaughter took place.

The Avedisian housing complex was situated in the very center of the village, giving them a little reprieve. The Kurds and their victims passed through the street below the house. Toomas and the other children and mothers would run to the windows and without exposing themselves, from the corners of the windows, watch the terror-stricken people as they marched along the street.

"Who are they taking now?" Toomas would ask. Pertoosh's face showed horror as she recognized the faces of beloved friends and their children.

During these days Pertoosh read often from the Bible, quoting God's promises. "Come, let us stop our moaning," she said. "We have a little time yet. God is still on His throne. He is still able to save us." Everyone knew that it would take a miracle to save them from death by the khandjar, but Pertoosh's faith never wavered. God *could* perform that miracle, she said.

She cooked, baked bread and continued to comfort the bereaved women in the days that followed. Giving the children a handful of raisins, she told them, "Go to the roof and play. And be careful."

Toomas, after the first shock of his father's death had passed, found that tears came easily. Often he asked Pertoosh, "Mama, why did God allow Papa to die?"

Taking his little face between her hands, Pertoosh replied, "Toomas, Papa is at peace. He is with God. Someday, we will see him. And then you will understand." She wiped his tears. For the present, Toomas could not understand, but when Pertoosh held him close and he felt the comfort of her soft bosom, somehow things seemed better.

Toomas would never forget an incident that happened during the days of the massacre. Ameh Nunia, with her four sisters, two little brothers, and her daughter, had been led to the shambles, never to return, so everyone thought. The Avedisian women had already cried and grieved for them.

One dark night while they slept, Pertoosh and the others were awakened by a faint cry. In the stillness of the night it came, "Hel—p! Hel—p! Hel—p!"

Pertoosh listened and heard it again. In a flash, she rose to her feet and flung open the door. A woman, kneeling, fell face down on the floor. Pertoosh knelt beside her. "Quick, Toomas, bring the lantern," she called.

Under the dim light of the lantern they saw the woman's face, lined with horror. Hair matted with caked blood, pieces of rags covering only part of her body, eyes wild with agony, she presented a ghastly vision.

A shocked look spread over Pertoosh's face. "Nunia, Nunia," she whispered in an incredulous voice. "We thought you were dead."

Was it really Ameh Nunia? Or were they seeing a ghost, Toomas wondered. Ameh Nunia had gone to the khandjar. *No one* came back. No one could escape. But it *was* Ameh Nunia.

Toomas felt tears of rebellion—savage hot tears. Ameh Nunia appeared more dead than alive. What had the cruel Kurds done to his half-blind, good, kind aunt? Ameh Nunia loved everyone and had never hurt anyone! "Oh, God," he cried, "strike them dead!"

Pertoosh turned to her son. "Hush, Toomas, you must not talk this way. This is the devil's work, and God will take care of them in His own good time."

Mama's words did nothing to appease Toomas's rage, and his feeling of rebellion increased as all through the night Pertoosh and Victoria nursed Ameh Nunia, who could only moan and groan in horror and pain.

The next day, after she had been cleaned and revived by loving hands, she was able, bit by bit, to tell the story. As she spoke, fresh tears came to bathe her face, and a haunted look came into her eyes. "My family—all gone!" Sobs wrenched her body. Pertoosh held her close, speaking words of comfort, but Ameh Nunia could not be comforted.

Between wails and sobs, her story came out. "They were swinging their khandjars left and right, cutting off heads, arms, legs. Everyone screaming. Blood flowing all over. Oh, it was awful! Hell itself can't be any worse.

"I fell to the ground unconscious. I knew nothing until I awakened and found myself among the dead. The Kurds must have thought I was dead, too."

"But how did you escape?" Pertoosh asked gently.

"When I realized I was not dead, I lay very still."

"You pretended you were dead," Pertoosh added.

"Yes." A wail escaped Nunia. "There I lay under the bodies of my sisters and brothers. I clutched my bare bosom, thinking a khandjar had pierced my heart. When I knew it hadn't, I rolled over in a pool of blood."

Hearing the gruesome details, everyone wept with Ameh Nunia. She went on, "I buried myself by rolling under several mangled bodies—I don't know who they were. I felt their blood and bare flesh and bones." She shuddered, and beads of sweat moistened her brow.

"How long did you stay there?" Pertoosh smoothed Nunia's hair.

"The Kurds came early the next morning to see if anyone moved, if anyone was still alive. If they found anyone with a breath of life, they finished them off with their khandjars. They are demons! I lay very still, I don't know how long. It must have been three or four days and nights. I passed out many times."

"But how did you manage to get past them to come here?"

"I crawled out at night—on my hands and knees. By day I hid in the culverts running with blood. I crawled at night hoping to reach your house."

Pertoosh wiped her tears. "You are safe now. God has spared your life, Nunia. You must rest now. Try to sleep some more." Ameh Nunia closed her eyes and fell into a fitful sleep from which she woke screaming and crying several times.

Much later, when she felt more revived, she was able to relate more of the Kurds' blood-curdling deeds.

Before the slaughter, at the shambles, they had tied together all the young girls, the voluptuous, the rosebuds of Armenian womanhood. They promised not to harm them. Of course the girls did not believe them, but were helpless.

Then, after all the women and children had been butchered, the Kurds turned their attention to their lovely young captives. One by one, they unroped and raped their victims, whose only defense was tooth and nail. The girls were devoured like helpless lambs in the paws of ferocious lions, and after the horrible invasion of their young bodies, they too were killed by the khandjars.

The tales of horror would never be forgotten by those who heard them, nor would the faith of the Christian people whose refusal to renounce their belief was their last act of obedience in this life. "Be thou faithful unto death and I will give thee a crown of life." (Revelation 2:10)

CHAPTER 17

"Mama, I Don't Want to Die!"

Generation after generation the Armenians had lived among the Moslems, whose proverbs were: "giaour's property is lawful to Moslems;" "giaour's neck is for the sword of Islam (Moslem);" "giaour's head belongs to the government, and his property to the public;" It is virtuous to drink giaour's blood;" "On the day of resurrection, the giaours shall grovel with their faces on the earth, while the Moslems shall walk erect and will be borne aloft on winged camels, white as snow."

Who could escape the plan of extermination, based as it was on these genocidal teachings?

As the day drew near for their execution, Pertoosh called upon God's name. Over and over she beseeched His power. "Lord, help us. Lord, help us," she prayed moment by moment.

Early one morning, as Toomas was looking out the window, he saw a Kurd standing on their roof. "Mama, Mama!" he exclaimed. "There's a Kurd on our roof."

Suddenly the inevitable took on an overwhelming reality. "Mama," Toomas cried with tears flowing down his frightened face, "I don't want to die! I want to live! I want to go to America to be with Aghegsanter. I want to be a doctor, like Amo Avedis and Amo Hagop."

Pertoosh, crushed to see her child pleading for the life that God had given him, could not control her own tears. What could she say to comfort him? She cupped his face in her hands.

"Toomas, if we are going to die, we must all go together as a family. You are a child. How could you live by yourself? How could you escape the Kurds?"

"No, no, Mama. I don't want to die! I'll hide from the Kurds." Toomas grabbed her leg and held on as though he would never let go.

Pertoosh felt the twist in her heart. Dear, brave Toomas—precious child. How she wanted to be able to grant him the right to live. She held him close to her heart, whispering, "Toomas, dear, Papa is calling us. He wants us to go to him. We will be all together."

Toomas's tears spilled on her skirt. "Mama, it isn't that I don't want to go to Papa. I *don't* want to die! I want to live!"

At that moment, Pertoosh, her heart wrenching with pain, offered her supplication, "Lord, save my child! Let him live!"

Toomas continued all day to sob and plead with his mother, "Please, Mama, don't let them take me. Don't let me die!"

Pertoosh searched her aching heart. What could she do? Only God could save Toomas. God could save them all. "Lord, help us. Thou art our refuge and our strength. Father in heaven, save our lives. If our lives are not to be spared, please, spare my child's life."

Hovsep did not share Toomas's desire to live. He said to his mother, "I want to die with the rest of you."

Toomas's persistent cries and pleas for his life continued to torture Pertoosh. What could she do? "Lord, if there is a way for Toomas to live, reveal it to me," she pleaded. While she cried and prayed, trying to comfort Toomas, a thought came to her, a faint thread of hope. She remembered the kind wealthy Kurd named Mustafa Agha. Garabed and Amo Hovaness had contracted and built his house, a beautiful villa on the outskirts of Hini.

During the days when the Kurds had come with pick and shovel to ransack their houses, looking for weapons, Mustafa Agha had repeatedly said to Pertoosh, *"Kerwa Pertoosh, mu-tursa, chickek chunnyoo toree, mu-tersa."* ("Friend Pertoosh, don't be afraid, we won't harm you. Don't be afraid.")

Desperate now to try to save Toomas's life, Pertoosh formulated a plan. She sent word with Hovsep to the Kurd telling him she wanted to meet with him in secret. Mustafa Agha agreed. Pertoosh told herself that her plan was a bold, wild grasp for her child's life. This Kurd had always shown the family the warmest friendliness. She would take advantage of their friendship. She would take a chance and go to him with her plea.

Under cover, lest she be recognized, she pulled her veil over her face and went to his house. Mustafa Agha invited her inside with utmost courtesy.

"Mustafa," she began (in Kurdish, of course), "you have always been our friend." She struggled to keep her voice from breaking. "Our time is short," she continued. A look of sympathy came into the Kurd's dark eyes.

Encouraged by the look, Pertoosh forced herself to go on. Pleading for her child's life, she made a proposition. "Mustafa, I will give you all our possessions of value—tonight—I will give you our gold coins, our silver, our bedding and furnishings." She paused. He must not hear the wild pounding of her heart. He must not see her fear.

The Kurd's eyes searched and pierced her own. "Yes, friend Pertoosh. What is your request?"

"My request is that you take my young son, Toomas. Keep him until after the massacre is over. I have a son who lives in America. I will give you his address. You must promise that you will inform him about Toomas, and he will send for him."

While she made her plea, she studied the man's face. The look of pleasure that had come over him—was it truly a desire to help or was it greed? All of Hini knew about the Avedisian family wealth, about their superior houses and exquisite furnishings.

Mustafa Agha replied quickly, "But, of course, Pertoosh. You know I would do anything to help you. I will take your son and do as you request."

For a second she saw him for what he was, a Moslem. Did not all Moslems hate Christians? How could she trust him? Yet he was their only hope. Perhaps, truly, this Kurd had a sympathetic heart. Perhaps, truly, he *could* be trusted. She had to take a chance.

An overwhelming sense of relief came over her. "Oh, thank you, thank you, Mustafa. You are kind. I will come tonight and bring the valuables." She could say no more and took her leave.

That night, long after the sun had set, Pertoosh gathered together the new silk sheets and comforters, never used, which she had stored away for Aghegsanter, as was the custom, to be his when he was married. This bedding she would take to the Kurd's house to be used as Toomas's bedding. She gathered some gold coins to take to Mustafa.

Toomas, happy with his mother's plan, made himself ready and said goodbye to Hovsep, Victoria and his grandparents, kissing their tears of sadness. He ran to the window and drew aside the curtains. "It's raining, Mama," he said.

The rain proved to be a blessing, for they were able to proceed unobserved to the Kurd's house.

Now the moment had come. How could she say goodbye to her baby—flesh of her flesh? She prayed silently for strength. Crushing Toomas against her bosom, she whispered, "No matter what happens, pray, Toomas. God will take care of you."

Toomas clung to her, his little arms wound around her neck. All at once he burst into sobs that tore her heart. "No, Mama, I changed my mind. I don't want to stay with the Kurds." He tightened his hold.

At that moment, she felt the worst agony of her life. She wanted to keep her child, for them to be together in death. But no, she must give him his one and only chance to escape the khandjar. She wiped his tears with a corner of her skirt. "Shh, now—they must not see you crying," she said, composing herself.

Once inside, she handed the gold coins to Mustafa and gave the beautiful bedding to his wife. "These are for Toomas," she said. "I will bring the silverware tomorrow." She turned to go. Before anyone could see her breaking heart, she brushed past the Kurd and his wife and out into the rain and blackness of the night.

When Toomas saw his mother vanish into the night, he could not hold back his sobs. Mustafa said, "You must not cry, Toomas. We will take care of you."

But Toomas could only break into fresh sobs. As much as he wanted to live, he could not bear separation from his mother. He had never before been away from her. He found the severance unbearable.

Mustafa's wife and ten-year-old daughter tried to comfort him, but to no avail. The Kurd's wife set a pan of food in the center of the floor. "Come, Toomas, sit down and have supper with us," she urged.

His angry stomach gave a growl. He sat on the floor just to be polite, and watched with downcast eyes as they enjoyed their supper, but he refused to take any for himself.

The young daughter watched Toomas, gave him a smile, then impulsively threw a small bunch of grapes into his lap.

Should he take them? After a little hesitation, he ate, gratefully. Better than nothing, he told himself.

After supper they had fun with him, teasing him because of his struggle with the Kurdish language. Although he could understand it, he could speak very little.

After they had had their fun, the wife said, "Toomas, you will sleep on the sofa." She led him to the sitting room, and left.

Toomas looked around the room. Where was the bedding his mother had brought for him to make him comfortable? Where were the sheets, blanket and pillow? He dared not ask.

He tried to go to sleep on the sofa, which felt hard as rocks under his back. A cold wind blew through the two open windows directly above the sofa. Without even one blanket, he shivered and cried. Where was his bedding? What had they done with it? For hours he lay on the sofa, stiff and cold.

At last he told himself he was going to find out where they had put his bedding. He tiptoed around and peeked into the Kurd's bedchamber. There it was! Mustafa and his wife lay comfortably under the bedding, while he was freezing from the bitter cold.

If they treat me like this, on the first night, he thought, how will they treat me later? Instantly, he made up his mind. As soon as the dawn came, he would run away. No one could stop him. He wanted only to be with his mother. The remaining hours were the longest in his life. Would the sun never rise?

As soon as the first rays of light glowed across the horizon, he tiptoed down the stairs, opened the door silently and ran. He had gone only a few yards when he saw a form rapidly approaching him. For a moment, terror struck him. Who could it be? Had Mustafa seen him and come out from another door? Or was it another Kurd who had discovered where he had been hidden?

The next moment, his fear vanished. In a flash, he *knew* who it was. His mother, Pertoosh! She had come after him. His feet flew as he ran to meet her, and he fell heavily into her open arms.

If time stopped now, he would have achieved the end desire of his short life—to be with his mother. Without a word, Pertoosh clasped him to her heart. Toomas longed to stay in her arms, buried in her bosom forever, with her hands, soft and loving, caressing his hair, soothing his heart.

"Toomas, my baby," she cried at last, smothering his face with kisses, her tears mingling with his. For a time, eternity stood still while the communion of love bound their hearts together.

Between tears, Toomas related the heartless treatment, ending his story with, "Mama, I would rather die with you than live with the Kurds."

"And I," said his mother, "waited all night for the dawn to come, so that I could come and claim you. You belong with us, Toomas." She held him close and kissed him again and again.

"Let us go home," she said tiredly. "God will take care of us."

Toomas believed his mother and his heart was at peace.

CHAPTER 18

Three Boys in the Straw

Pertoosh and Toomas hurried through the streets of Hini. They must reach home before the sun blazed with its glory to light up the day. No one must see them. In the background surrounding Hini, the lofty peaks were like sentinels standing at attention. Mother and son broke into a run and did not stop until they reached their house.

Both Pertoosh and Toomas had a strong premonition that this was the day the Kurds would come for all of them. All the aunts, with their children, were now staying with them. They had not dared to stay in their own homes, and they needed Pertoosh's strength and comfort.

Knowing the day of their doom was upon them, Toomas's two aunts, Abajee Khanum and Abajee Shooshan, came up with a plan to save one child from each family. Even if their plan, born out of desperation and confusion, worked, the children still might not be able to survive. Yet, at least for Toomas's sake, they would take that chance, perhaps one in ten thousand.

With the pain of Toomas's experience with the Kurds so fresh in her mind, Pertoosh said, "What chance do you think Looderr, only four, Aram, only five, and Toomas, only six years old, will have to survive among the Kurds, without us?"

Hearing this, Toomas cried with tears in his eyes, "Mama, I'll take care of Aram and Looderr. I didn't want to stay with the Kurds, but I still don't want to die. Please, Mama, let us live."

Pertoosh stifled the anguish in her heart as she listened to her child—hardly more than a baby himself, yet willing to take care of his young cousins. During the past two months he had seen and experienced the horrors which all of them had been exposed to. He seemed more like an adult than a child.

She had to give him the chance to live, as flimsy as it might be. Once the decision had been made, the three mothers went about preparing the children and giving instructions. "Toomas," Pertoosh pointed out, "here is the secret hiding place for our gold coins, silver money, jewelry, clothes and some important documents." She pointed to a board on the wall which Garabed had removed and replaced when they had hidden the Bible.

"Do not tell *anyone* about this hiding place until you are in safe hands." In her heart, she believed God would spare Toomas and the children. And in His mercy He could save them all!

Abajee Khanum and Abajee Shooshan, amid confusion, gave instructions to their little ones. "Stay close to Toomas. Do what he tells you, and never tell anyone where we have hidden our valuables," they said.

Pertoosh wrote on a slip of paper, saying, "This is the name and address of Aghegsanter in America." Very carefully, reinforcing every stitch, she sewed the piece of paper under a patch on the back of Toomas's undershirt, saying, "Never part with this shirt, until you have reached your brother." Then she handed him his tiny Bible, the New Testament she and Garabed had given him on his third birthday. "Keep this with you always." She bent to kiss Toomas, her eyes brimming with tears.

Toomas placed both arms around her waist. "Yes, I will," he promised.

Then the mothers told the children their hiding place would be down in the darkest cellar underneath their houses. "You will hide in the straw in back of the food storage vessels," Pertoosh told them. "You will not have to worry about food, for the vessels are filled with dried fruit, nuts, corn, rice, and everything else."

After smothering the children with countless kisses, blessing and prayers, the three mothers took their little ones to the cellar and settled them among the storage vessels.

After Pertoosh said goodbye once again to Toomas, she lifted her heart and committed him to God's care. The boys would get along together, she told herself. Toomas was a bright child, with the wisdom of an older boy. The three cousins had always played together, and the younger ones would mind Toomas, for he had worn out more shirts than they (an Armenian expression).

With their mothers gone, Looderr and Aram began to cry. "Quiet," said Toomas. "You're going to be all right. I'll take care of you." He stepped out of the straw and dipped his hand into a storage vessel, bringing up a handful of raisins as he had often seen his grandmother, Sopig Mama, do. The boys stopped crying and ate the raisins.

But after they had finished the raisins, Aram began to whimper and Looderr began to cry, "I want my mama." He covered his face.

"Stop crying, Looderr, and I'll tell you some Jesus stories," Toomas said. Looderr looked up with tear-filled eyes, wiping away the tears with chubby little fists. Aram stopped whimpering and waited.

The boys listened quietly, for Toomas was a dramatic story-teller. He told them stories about Jesus that Pertoosh had taught him—how He once was a little baby born in the straw, just like they were occupying right now. He told them how Jesus took little children on His knees and loved them. "Jesus will take care of us," he promised.

Under a dim ray of light that filtered from a small window, Toomas "read" to them from his small Bible. Since he could not read the words, he read only the letters of the alphabet.

An hour went by. It seemed an eternity to Toomas. What was going on upstairs? Had the Kurds come yet? Mama had said she was sure they would come, for theirs was the next house in line.

When he could not endure one more moment of suspense, he said, "Aram and Looderr, you stay right here. I'm going to lift the trap door and peek. I want to see what's going on." He put his finger to his lips. "Be very quiet and I'll be right back."

Very carefully, he climbed out of his nest in the straw, and tiptoed to the ladder leading to the trap door of the living room floor. Slowly and watchfully, he pushed the heavy door with all his might, using both hands and head, opening the door just a few inches.

Instantly, he lowered the door—just in the knick of time! A Kurd, rifle in hand, a satisfied look on his face (for he was leaving a vacant house behind), had just turned and was walking to the door which led outside.

"Whew!" Toomas wiped his face with his sleeve. "Lucky for me. If I had stuck my head up a second sooner, he would have seen me."

At that moment, Pertoosh's words rang in his ears, "God will take care of you." God indeed had already taken care of them.

He plunged into the straw with Aram and Looderr. Trying to act cheerful because he had not been caught, yet crying in his heart because the Kurds had taken his beloved mother and family away to die, he cried in a high pitched voice, "The Kurds don't know we are here. They are leaving the house. We are *not* going to die. Do you hear? We are *not* going to die. We are going to live! We are going—"

All of a sudden he wondered, without his mother, who was after all his reason for living, did he really want to live?

He buried his head in the straw and cried.

CHAPTER 19

Miraculous Escape

Upstairs again, after leaving the little boys in the cellar, Pertoosh watched from the window, sure that the Kurds would come soon. Her thoughts went to the three boys, hardly more than babies, hiding in the straw. God in His mercy could spare their lives. "Lord," she prayed, "a miracle. Save their lives."

She knelt on the floor where the two aunts and Victoria were praying. "A miracle, Lord," she beseeched, with agony in her heart and faith on her lips. "And Lord, what good are our children without their mothers? Lord, they need us. Please, a miracle, for all of us!"

The sound of heavy footsteps stomping on the stairs brought them quickly to their feet. Pertoosh's heart sank. The enemy had come. Their hour was here. She said to Abajee Khanum and Abajee Shooshan and Victoria, "Now remember, do not move hastily. Be as slow as you dare."

The children began to cry, clinging to their mothers. Hovsep stayed close to his mother, his eyes flashing hatred for the Kurds. One of the aunts, Abajee Khanum, Amo Krikor's wife, wailed, "Oh, if only Krikor were here. Why did he have to go to Lidja?"

"You forget," Pertoosh replied. "The Kurds called him to make some plows for them. How could he refuse?"

71

"Yes," cried Abajee Khanum, "that's why they haven't massacred him yet. Oh, if he were here, they would not take me."

"Courage," Pertoosh said, as she moved toward the door. "God is able to save us."

The door burst open and several Kurdish soldiers, rifles in hand, walked in. "Everyone out," they barked. They went from room to room looking for occupants and striking terror in everyone's heart.

Speaking very calmly, Pertoosh said, "Our three families are the only ones here. If you don't believe me, look around. On the roof. See for yourselves."

Dada Khazzar sat on a stool, not moving, his eyes fixed in a stare. He was already in a state of shock and nothing seemed to penetrate his brain.

The Kurds turned away. They searched every corner, kicking bedding into the air, overturning stools, tossing pillows, leaving nothing unturned. Butting the women and children with their rifles, they herded them, trembling and terror-stricken, down the stairs.

But not Pertoosh. She would not be hurried. She pretended she had forgotten a baby's milk bottle or a blanket. She ran out on the veranda to look for a shawl. Ignoring the Kurd who had stayed behind to personally escort her out, she rushed from room to room, looking for something that could not be found, pretending frustration.

During all the confusion fifteen minutes had elapsed. The death procession had gained fifteen precious minutes, she told herself, after the others had been forced outside. While pretending frustration, her heart bled for a miracle. "Lord, help us," she prayed over and over.

At last, the Kurdish soldier, his dark eyes flashing from his broad face with its high cheekbones, fingered his khandjar and spat out, "Leave *now*, or I will finish you right here!"

One look at his face told Pertoosh she had used all the time she dared.

Downstairs she joined the others—all members of her family—who had been driven into an adjoining courtyard. A full hour had passed and the Kurdish soldiers were impatient to lead the procession to the shambles. They mounted their horses.

The women cried heart-rending sobs, and the children, seeing their mothers' torments, cried harder. Pertoosh thought of the three boys in the cellar and again beseeched God for help.

She looked around at the house that had given her many years of happiness, where her children had been born and Garabed had been there to love all of them. For a moment, she felt a terrible weakness. Would her heart break right here? No, no, she must not, for the sake of the others, show any weakness. Turning to face them all, she called, "Let us not give up hope."

The women prayed in Armenian, which the Kurdish soldiers did not understand. A soldier shouted, "Let's go. Into the street, everyone."

They were about to exit from the courtyard into the street. The Kurdish chieftain stood behind the group of weeping, wailing, praying women. He swore because it had taken a full hour to vacate the Avedisian families. Full of rage and impatience, he uttered curse after curse upon the giaours.

The procession had formed and was about to proceed in the street when, suddenly, everyone stopped in his tracks.

"Move on, move on," shouted a soldier.

"No, no," Pertoosh called above the soldier's shout. What was that? A Kurd bearing a piece of paper in his hand had made his way through the crowd and was walking toward the chieftain in the back.

Could it be? Pertoosh asked herself. "Dear God. Let it be what I think. Let it be. Save us!" Over and over she uttered her agonized prayer.

By now the air had become electrified. The wailing and sobbing had ceased. A dynamic current seemed to flow over those who had been doomed to die, who had already died in spirit. Hope, faith, optimism—all these reflected on the faces of those who were being led to the slaughter. A revitalized flow of life had already begun to flow through arteries that had congealed with terror. Looks of hope replaced the looks of despair.

The Kurd with the piece of paper reached the chieftain and handed him the message. As he read it, a look of incredible rage spread over his features. Then he spoke the words, interspersed with many oaths, that gave these giaours the right to live instead of die.

"Go back to your homes. The *madoor* (mayor) has spared your lives." He spat on the ground, uttered another oath, saying he could not understand, slapped his horse and galloped away. The soldiers followed him, all uttering loud oaths.

Cries of unutterable happiness and thankfulness pierced the air. The children shouted for joy, while their mothers took them and jumped up and down with ecstacy. Praise God! They would not die!

Pertoosh dropped to her knees right there in the street. Too overcome for words, her heart too full for any more emotion, she could only lift her thoughts, "Lord God, you are great. You are merciful. You have performed the miracle. Thank you. Oh, thank you." Then she let the tears spill and did not care who saw.

When her tears had subsided, she knew why she had been inspired to delay the Kurds. God had been guiding all the way.

And Toomas and his cousins—they were going to live. God had answered their prayers!

As long as she lived, she would never forget the miraculous manner in which God had saved them. As long as a breath remained in her body she would praise His name. She had witnessed the great power and glory of God. The sword of Islam would never touch her.

Safely inside the house, Pertoosh and the others wondered. God had indeed performed the miracle, but how had it come about? Why did the madoor decide to spare the lives of the Avedisian women and children?

The next day, Amo Krikor returned from Lidja, the nearby village where he had gone at the request of the Kurds, to make plows for them. Amo Krikor, as an outstanding artist and craftsman, was in great demand by the Kurds. His life had thus far been spared because they had deemed his services irreplaceable. The Kurds were skilled only at breeding cattle, horses, sheep and goats, and were not craftsmen of any kind.

Amo Krikor supplied the answer to the women's questions. After rejoicing with all of them because they were alive, because they had escaped the horrible khandjar, he told them how it had happened.

"As you know," he began, "the Kurds in Lidja sent for me to go there and make some wooden plows. I told them, very humbly, of course, that I was very grateful that my life had been spared for the purpose of making plows for them." He paused once more, savoring the memory.

"Then I offered to make plows for them the rest of my life, if they would spare my family. I told them that without my family I would not want to live. I would commit suicide."

Pertoosh searched his face. A kind man who loved his family with a passion, he *would* rather die than live without them, she believed.

"Did they agree right away?" she asked.

"Not at first. The madoor hesitated, especially when I told him that we three families lived together in one complex, and that all were my family." He looked around the room from one family member to the other—his family, whose lives he had pleaded for.

"What made him change his mind?" his wife asked.

Amo Krikor looked puzzled. "I must have looked very frail and helpless to him. What are my hundred and thirty-five pounds compared with his, maybe, two hundred? He must have thought I wouldn't live long anyway. What harm could I do? (Actually, Amo Krikor outlived many a Kurd, living more than ninety years.)

"Besides, they need you more than ever now," Pertoosh said.

"That's true. It took a long time for him to concede, while I died a thousand deaths. Finally, he accepted my proposition and sent a written requisition to the madoor of Hini."

"It came just in time, Krikor!" his wife cried, tears of joy spilling on her face. "A few minutes later would have been too late."

"Thank God. Thank God." Krikor bowed his head with gratitude.

"God was leading us all the way," Pertoosh added. "It was He who inspired me to stall the Kurds fifteen minutes more."

All agreed that God in His mercy had performed a wonderful miracle for them.

CHAPTER 20

"Mohammedanize? Never!"

Down in the cellar, shortly after the piece of paper had arrived giving the order to spare the lives of the Avedisian families, Toomas heard footsteps above. Someone was walking upstairs in the living room! His heart thumped so hard he thought it would jump right out of its place.

Dear God, was it a Kurd? Had he seen Toomas out of the corner of his eye, after all? Why hadn't he waited before opening the trap door? Why had he been so anxious to go have a look? He began to tremble. Aram and Looderr began to cry as loudly as they could.

76

"Shh," Toomas cried, "or I'll have to plug your mouths!"

While he talked, the trap door opened. "Oh, my God, he did see me," Toomas cried. Wild terror crept over him like the wave of a stormy sea.

In his mind's eye he saw the horrid khandjar at work swiftly yet leisurely, cutting his ears off first, his nose next, his tongue off at its root, and finally, his head off its axis! He saw these members, one after another, falling to the ground in a pool of blood.

Paralyzed with fear, unable to move, he fastened his eyes on the trap door. He remembered Mama's words, "Always call on the name of Jesus when in trouble."

"Jesus, save us!" He placed his arms around his little cousins as though to protect them. They were sobbing. All the Kurds in Hini must have heard them!

Now a pair of legs was coming down the stairs, a voluminous skirt covering them! Wait! That wasn't a Kurd. It was a woman! The woman turned her face. Toomas saw her, a beautiful smile on her face. "It's cousin Beatrice!" he shouted, letting go of the boys.

"Toomas, Looderr, Aram, we're free! We don't have to die. We are—all of us in the family—going to live!" She hugged and kissed the boys, one by one. Was he dreaming, or was it true? Toomas asked himself.

The boy's happiness took on a pair of wings. One moment death had faced them. The next moment life had been given them.

"It was a miracle," Beatrice said. "Let's go upstairs and your mothers will tell you all about it." Still thinking it was a dream, Toomas nodded.

The little boys jumped out of their nests of straw and dashed up the stairs. There were their mothers running to meet them with outstretched arms. What a moment it was! There was laughing and crying all at once. Time could just as well have stopped for Toomas.

Only twenty-four Armenian families remained in Hini, after the Kurds had completed their terrible work.

Then, as if the Kurds, with their diabolical actions, had not been efficient enough to exterminate the Armenians, nature came to their aid with a pestilential khandjar.

A disease, highly infectious, broke out throughout Hini. One little girl, without a father or mother, contracted the disease. No one wanted any part in taking care of the child. Pertoosh went to visit the child, and when she saw her alone, neglected and dying, her heart filled with compassion and she brought the little girl to her house. They placed her in the cellar, away from the rest of the families.

Without a doctor in the village, and without medicine or anyone with medical knowledge, the child died within a few days.

The dreaded disease was cholera.

Now more tragedy struck Pertoosh's family. Seven family members followed one another in death. Among them were Victoria's two chubby little boys and four of Toomas's cousins, including Looderr and Aram, his mates in the straw.

Pertoosh felt yet another unbearable break in her heart. Toomas could not be consoled for his cousins. Hovsep wept with the others. Victoria's grief was inexpressible. First a widow, now childless, she cried, "I should have died with them."

The grief-stricken mothers wrapped their children, took their shovels and buried them in the Armenian cemetery. "If only we had a doctor," they wailed.

Pertoosh tried to comfort them as well as herself. "God has for some good reason permitted our little ones to be laid to rest. Perhaps it is to spare them from a fate worse than this."

At last, the massacre came to an end, and cholera took its last victim. Now thirty-four women and children, out of four thousand Armenians in Hini, remained.

Thirty-four out of four thousand! Even with such a small number, Pertoosh could praise God. "Christianity has not been destroyed," she said. "There are still a few Christians left."

Throughout the country, the Kurds and Chachans had been responsible for the genocide of one and one-half million Armenians. The infamous, unspeakable deed of the Turkish Mohammedans, who had massacred a whole nation of Christians, would go down indelibly in history.

Pertoosh, with the rest of the thirty-four survivors, now wondered what the Kurds would do next. They were soon to learn that the Kurds were not through with them, but had already formulated a plan to force the few survivors into Mohammedanism. When this tyrannical plan came to light, Pertoosh exclaimed, "Mohammedanize us? Never!"

So this was why their lives had been exempted. But to renounce Christianity and embrace Mohammedanism was unthinkable! No one among the family would yield!

The Kurds began by sending their *mullahs* (holy men) to the

Armenian homes. For the first time since the massacre the survivors were treated with a note of kindness.

The holy men said kindly, "First, you will be given names. You may have the privilege of choosing your own names."

While Pertoosh determined in her heart that the Mohammedans would never succeed with the plan to convert them, she listened to the mullah, who said, "Pertoosh, we know you will never accept our faith, but if you will go along with us and listen to us as we present our sacred Koran, we will continue to exempt your life and that of your family."

Pertoosh wanted to reply, "No, we don't want to listen to your Koran. It was God who spared our lives." Instead, confident that nothing he said could change their minds, she nodded. She knew they had no other choice.

As far as the Armenians were concerned, the selection of Kurdish names was only a farce. Toomas chose the name of Shookree because it was the most heroic name in Turkey. Hovsep assumed Youseff for his name. Victoria selected Emma, and Pertoosh became Faatma.

The mullah next began to teach them the symbols and meanings of the Moslem *namaz* (prayers). Then he read a few paragraphs from the Koran. When he asked them to repeat the prayers, Pertoosh asked, "Since we cannot pronounce the Turkish words, may we say them in Armenian?"

The mullah did not understand the Armenian language, although, in reality, Pertoosh and the others did understand the Turkish language. So while the mullah prayed his Mohammedan prayers in Turkish, they prayed in Armenian, "Lord, help us. We will never deny thee, Jesus. Almighty God, you know our hearts." The mullah, thinking they were repeating his prayers after him, smiled contentedly.

What a farce, thought Pertoosh. "Dear God, forgive us for even listening."

After a few days of exposing the family to the Koran and the Moslem prayers, the mullah suggested they go to the Mosque and watch how the Mohammedans worshipped their Allah. Though they went several times, the experience did as little to change their convictions as any of the mullah's other attempts.

After a few weeks, the mullah, seeing his efforts had not borne results, ceased to attempt to Mohammedanize the remaining thirty-four Armenians who "had not bowed the knee to Baal" (Bible quotation). God had other plans for them.

Now that the fear of having to convert to Mohammedanism
had passed, a new problem arose for the Armenians. The Kurds,
who practiced polygamy, began to try to ensnare the young
Armenian girls into marriage.

Would they never cease their atrocities? Pertoosh was revolted
at the very idea, for Armenians held marriage as a sacrament.
They loathed and looked down on the Kurds' practice of polygamy. She, for one, would have no part of it. But there was
Victoria. Would they try to force her?

Victoria remained firm. She would not affiliate herself with a
Kurd in marriage, even if it meant her life.

A few, preferring death, committed suicide by jumping into the
well in their yards and drowning. Some were wed forcibly,
against their will. Three girls from the remainder of the Avedisian family, including Zaabel, Amo Hovaness's daughter, and
cousin Voto, believing they were doing the right thing, sacrificed
themselves by marrying the Kurds who came courting.

"Why are you doing this?" Pertoosh asked with tears in her
eyes.

"Because if we do not, you will all die," Zaabel had replied.
"The Armenian race must be preserved," she said, drying her own
tears. "And I promise I will *never* become Mohammedan."

CHAPTER 21

Escape from Hini

Pertoosh and her family found life without fathers, mothers,
uncles, aunts, brothers and sisters, sons and daughters, utterly
intolerable. For them, Hini, once their beloved treasure, had
turned into a place of nightmares, of haunting, searing mem-
ories.

How could they continue to live among the Kurds who had

committed the atrocities against them? On the other hand, where could they go? While it was true that the Avedisian family was wealthy, most of their wealth, one million dollars, was tied up in estates in and surrounding Hini. And although Pertoosh had hidden the family jewelry and gold and silver coins before the Kurds had come, she could not help but wonder how far these would go.

While these questions troubled her mind, she thought of her son in America. If only there were some way to reach him—but now that was not possible, since the war had stopped all communication with him. "Aghegsanter, my son, you are blessed among men, for you are in the land of the free," she spoke her thoughts aloud. If only there were a way she could take her children and find her way to that blessed land. "Dear God," she prayed, "you are gracious and all powerful. Help us to find a way."

Whenever she spoke of Aghegsanter before Toomas, he would say, "Mama, I want to go to America and become a doctor like my uncles are."

She would kiss him on the forehead and say, "May the Lord give you the desire of your heart."

After a few months, the Kurds began to show their regrets and some friendliness, and soon afterwards, a turn of events came about to give Pertoosh new hope.

Zaabel, her niece who had married a wealthy young Kurd, suddenly found herself a widow. Her husband's middle-aged brother, also wealthy, highly respected, and a man of letters and position, came from Diyarbekir to attend the funeral.

After the funeral, the *Effendi* (Master), as he was called, went to Pertoosh and stated his intention to marry Zaabel. Very respectfully, he said, "Pertoosh, as you know, it is our custom to marry the widow of a dead brother. I shall marry Zaabel, with your kind permission, and take her with me to Diyarbekir."

Pertoosh shrank from the very idea, for this man already had a Turkish wife. Yet she knew the reason for the custom. To take Zaabel as his wife would preserve the family inheritance.

The Effendi, somehow, was unlike the rest of the Kurds. He held a great deal of respect for Pertoosh's family. In fact, he had shown genuine concern and sorrow for what had been done to the Armenians. Rumor had it that somewhere in this man's family ran a strain of Armenian blood.

He had looked Pertoosh straight in the eye and said, "Pertoosh, it is my belief that since the Armenians were the first race in the world to accept Christianity, someday the Armenians will dominate the Moslems."

Looking into his piercing dark eyes, Pertoosh had seen a ray of sincerity. "If you believe that, Effendi," she said, "why do you not renounce Mohammedanism and embrace Christianity?"

"Yes, Pertoosh, most assuredly, when the time comes, if that happens in my lifetime, I will become a Christian."

"But, Effendi, why not now?"

"Oh, no. I cannot do such a thing now. My people would devour me whole, body and soul."

"You could leave Turkey, Effendi. You could go to the land of the free—a place called America."

The Effendi smiled and adjusted his turban. "Yes, I know about America. But I cannot leave my position in Turkey."

Pertoosh was well aware of his situation. The Effendi was a prominent man in Turkey. His office in Diyarbekir as provost of the entire educational department of the *vilayet* (province), made his name a law—an object of worship. His title bespoke volumes. His very dress, mannerisms, and speech were above reproach. While Pertoosh wondered what else to say to this man of great importance, he assured her, "I feel sure that someday in the future, I will, because of my convictions, have to leave Turkey."

Pertoosh searched her soul for the right thing to say to him about Zaabel. If she objected, he could take Zaabel forcibly. He had been most respectful, most courteous, in giving Pertoosh the opportunity to give her blessings. And Zaabel had already indicated her willingness to insure their future by marrying him. How could Pertoosh dissuade her now? Besides, in her heart Pertoosh felt gratitude to this man who had shown them consideration and respect. She concluded that she was helpless to prevent the marriage. Then a bright thought crossed her mind. Somehow, she felt that through association with this man, God was opening a door for their future!

She would take advantage of his friendship and family relationship. Here was a golden opportunity! She would make him an offer. After all, Zaabel still belonged to them, and the Effendi had indicated that he wished for the family's permission to marry her. Pertoosh had a right to state her desire.

"Effendi," she began, "we are willing to give you Zaabel as your wife, if you will consent to help us."

The Effendi smiled graciously and waved a hand. "Yes, Pertoosh. What is your request?"

"As you know, it is most difficult for my family and me to live in Hini now since—since—"

A look of understanding came into the Effendi's kind eyes. "Yes, Pertoosh, I certainly do understand your position."

"We would like to leave Hini, but we have no place to go. We would like shelter in your mansion for a time, until such time as we can find our own way again. We would like to come to live in Diyarbekir, if this meets with your approval."

Without hesitation, the Effendi replied, "If that is what you want, Pertoosh, you come and live in my home as long as you want to."

Pertoosh felt that a great weight had been lifted off her shoulders. She could not suppress her excitement and gratitude. "Effendi, you are a wonderful, kind man. Will you give us your promise?" She believed this good man would keep his promise.

"On my honor, Pertoosh," he smiled, showing pearly white teeth and great pleasure in her consent to give him Zaabel.

"God bless you," Pertoosh whispered. God had indeed opened the way.

She assured him that some way, somehow, they would find transportation to Diyarbekir very soon. "I'll be waiting," he said.

After the Effendi's departure, Pertoosh at once went to work to plan their departure. How would her family—Victoria, Hovsep, Toomas, and she herself—get to Diyarbekir, a distance of two days' rapid travel by horse? The rest of the Avedisian family agreed to stay in Hini until the way opened for them to leave, and Pertoosh promised that as soon as it was feasible she would send for them.

Pertoosh thought of the Kurd who had married her niece Voto after the massacre. He owned horses. She would go to him and ask for help.

At first he showed reluctance. Pertoosh saw that she must make it a lucrative transaction for him. "If you will loan us horses for my family, I will pay you gold coins."

"No, no, Pertoosh. It is too great a risk. What will the madoor say if he finds it was I who helped you get out of Hini?" He shook his head.

"I will give you jewelry. Please, I beg you, do us this great favor," Pertoosh pleaded.

"It's too great a risk." His words had a ring of finality, yet Pertoosh felt that a greater bounty could change his mind, so she offered him more gold coins. Though still protesting that it was a great risk, the young Kurd agreed.

"Give us one day," Pertoosh said, "to get our things together."

With the help of the children, she packed clothing, tools and other necessities. Hovsep went with her to the basement where she had hidden some of the jewelry and helped her dig it up. She sewed the diamond necklaces, gold pins and earrings, and jeweled rings into a little sack, and sewed the sack on a belt around her waist, under her voluminous skirt. With Hovsep's help, she removed the board in the living room that Garabed had so ingeniously replaced when he hid the large family Bible. She retrieved the large book of sacred scriptures that had been in the family for over one hundred years.

"Victoria, wrap this Bible very carefully. It will go with us wherever we go," she said, handing the book to her daughter.

Pertoosh had also hidden a quantity of gold and silver coins with the Bible. Now she took them out and sewed them on a large strip which Victoria placed on a belt around her waist as her mother had done. There were silver belts which they wrapped and hid around their waists.

The next night they said goodbye to Dada Khazzar, who still stared blankly, Sopig Mama, who shed many tears, and the rest of the family with whom they had grown very close. "Do not worry," Pertoosh assured them. "As soon as there is a place for you to stay, we will send for you."

After many blessings and tears, they parted. The young Kurd waited in the moonlight with the horses—one for Pertoosh, one for Victoria, and one for Hovsep—and a lowly donkey for little Toomas.

They packed the animals and made their exodus, leaving behind their ancestral village, where they had had so much happiness and so much sorrow. They left behind their lands and possessions, never again to return.

Pertoosh said, "We must not look back."

When they arrived in Diyarbekir at the Effendi's house, they found his valet had prepared a place for them in the servants' quarters, and they were full of gratitude.

Hardly had they alighted from the horses and carried their scant possessions to their rooms than the Effendi's Turkish wife, Fima, came breezing in. Holding her chin up with the air of a haughty queen, she inquired, "Are things well?" Her eyes zig-zagged around the room, searing most of all through Pertoosh. Pertoosh read her mind. Fima could not hide the hatred she felt for the giaours.

After she had left, Victoria spoke her thoughts. "She hated us not only because we are Armenians, but because she is jealous of Zaabel."

"Yes," replied Pertoosh, "she sees Zaabel as her rival, intruding in her life, sharing her husband and possessions. It would be difficult for any first wife not to feel this way."

Instead of extending a welcome to Pertoosh and her children, the jealous wife did all in her power to make them feel uncomfortable and unwanted. That evening when the Effendi came home from his office, he went to Pertoosh and explained, "I must tell you, Pertoosh, that since I brought Zaabel home as my wife, Fima has been doing everything in her power to get Zaabel out of here. And I am sure, now that you have arrived, she will try harder."

"I am truly sorry for her," Pertoosh said, with genuine feelings.

"Oh, but you are not to pay heed to her," the Effendi warned. "I have instructed Zaabel not to tolerate her actions. She is not to be lenient with her. She has my permission to chasten her should she make any insults, verbal or otherwise."

Zaabel, however, thought better of retaliating against the jealous wife directly. Instead, when the Effendi came home at night, she reported Fima's actions to him.

In this instance the Effendi attended to Fima personally. Rolling up his sleeves and taking the cane he always carried, he entered his Turkish wife's private rooms. The cries and pleas that filled the air convinced those who heard that the Effendi was administering, without clemency, a most sound beating.

Yet day after day, the jealous woman displayed her vicious hatred for Zaabel and her family. And day after day, they saw the Effendi enter her room with his cane and give her her punishment.

Watching the poor woman receive such unrelenting and regular chastisement evoked a wave of sympathy from Pertoosh. She rationalized to the children, "It is an unbearable situation for her to confront her rival daily—right here in her own home."

"Yes, it must kill her to see a giaour become her equal—a wife for the Effendi. And if Zaabel has sons, the sons of a giaour will have the same rights as her own," Victoria added.

Pertoosh shook her head. "Of course, the Effendi is only exercising the right given him by the Prophet Mohammed. He may bring as many wives into his home as he wishes." A sad feeling came over her. "This is not God's way," she added.

While they talked they heard a scuffle and the sound of a child crying. "Why, that sounds like Toomas." Pertoosh ran to see what was going on. Toomas came running to meet her and fell into her arms.

Pertoosh held him close. "What happened, Toomas?" She smoothed his tousled hair. "Have you been playing with the Effendi's son again?"

"Yes." Toomas brushed his tears with a small fist.

"But I told you, Toomas, not to play with the 'cry baby.'"

"I know, Mama, but I'm cooped up all day in the courtyard and there's no one else to play with. Besides, when he fell down and skinned his knee, I was on the other side of the fountain." Fresh sobs escaped him.

"But why are you crying?" Pertoosh asked.

"Because the Effendi's wife beat me!" Toomas rolled up his sleeve and showed the angry bruise on his arm.

Matters became worse a few months later, when Pertoosh sent for the other members of the family, with the Effendi's permission. Now there were sixteen people packed in a twelve by fourteen room!

Still, all agreed, anything was bearable, for they were alive!

CHAPTER 22

The Conquerors

While grateful to the Effendi that his kindness offered a new start in life, Pertoosh had to face the fact that all sixteen members of her family must provide their own living.

At first she used their gold coins to buy food. But as she saw their funds rapidly dwindling, she knew that efforts had to be made to earn money. What could any of them do? In Hini there had always been plenty of money, food and whatever was needed to live. Dada Khazzar and Sopig Mama had always attended to and provided the families with needed funds, and all of the men of the family had had skills. But now, what could they do?

If only Garabed were here! A pang of grief struck her heart. She wiped away the tears that welled. No, she would not indulge in them.

Toomas asked, "Mama, what shall we do for money?" Then in a few moments he shouted, "I know! Hovsep can make knolleens and then he can sell them!"

That sounded like a good idea. Since knolleens were used extensively outdoors on muddy days and during religious ablutions, there was always a demand for them. And Hovsep had acquired a skill in making them.

Eager to be of help, Hovsep agreed. "I'll make them, Mama, but I won't sell them. I'm not a salesman."

"But Hovsep," Pertoosh pleaded, "it will do us no good just to make them. You must go out and sell them. We need money very badly."

"No," Hovsep insisted, frowning. "I am not a salesman, and I won't go door to door."

Once again, Toomas came to the rescue. "Mama," he cried, jumping up and down. "I can go from door to door and sell them. Please, Mama, let me do that. You'll see, I can sell!"

Pertoosh looked at her little man. If only Garabed could see and hear him now! Toomas radiated such enthusiasm that she decided to let him try. "All right, Toomas. If Hovsep will make them, you will sell them."

"Yes," agreed Hovsep. "I will make them, if Toomas will sell them. I'm glad I brought my adz, saw and file!"

And so began Toomas's first endeavor as a salesman. Sometimes Pertoosh would accompany him, disguised in veil and *charsheff* (a tunic to cover the entire body, from head to feet), standing a distance away. Toomas went from house to house, peddling the knolleens. Holding one clog in each hand, he struck their bottoms together for effect, making noise. At the same time, he yelled at the top of his voice, "Knollee—eee—een, knoll—eee—een! *A la knolleen! Guoozal der boo knolleen!*" (Good knolleens! Beautiful knolleens!) Toomas yelled his wares in Turkish, and sold many pairs.

One day he found himself in a very wealthy Turkish section of the city with a beautifully designed pair of knolleens. Pertoosh had said, "You are *not* to part with them unless you are offered a very good price. These knolleens must bring us enough money to buy food for several days."

"Yes, Mama," he had replied, thoroughly enjoying his role as a salesman and breadwinner.

As he walked along the street, a Turkish woman eyed the knolleens and asked Toomas if they were for sale. Taking them out of his hands, she said, "I'll be back," and vanished into the house. She had lured him into the courtyard. Thinking she had gone inside to show the clogs to someone or to get money, Toomas waited patiently. Twenty minutes passed, with no sign of the woman.

Toomas felt his patience vanishing. Why was she taking so long? He rapped at the door and rattled it. When there was no response, he opened the door and walked inside. Since there was no one in the room, he sat against the wall on the floor and waited. Surely she would come soon!

Suddenly another woman emerged from an inner room and, seeing Toomas, yelled in an angry, unkind voice, "Be off! Get out of here!"

"But, I want my knolleens!" Toomas said, and started to cry. The woman denied any knowledge of them. She slammed the door and disappeared.

Toomas remained glued to the floor for another twenty minutes. She had better bring those knolleens back! Another twenty

minutes passed, and the first woman, the one who had snatched
his knolleens, appeared. Letting out a barrage of turbulent
words, she threatened, "If you do not leave this minute, I will
throw you out personally."

Toomas would not budge. He remembered Mama's words,
"Those shoes must buy food for us for several days."

The woman went inside a room. Thinking that perhaps she
had gone for a weapon or more help, Toomas finally decided he
had better vanish.

He never forgot the experience that had cost a pair of beautiful
wooden clogs—and food that would have lasted for a few days.

Besides food, the family needed fuel to burn in the fireplace
and for cooking. Wood and dried dung were used for this purpose, but since the latter was unobtainable in the city, they had to
find wood. Wood was sold at the market place, but the family
could not afford to buy it, so Pertoosh said, "You boys will have
to go outside the city and find wood."

Toomas, Hovsep, and their cousins, eager to help, agreed to
go. They went outside the walls of the city, down to the banks of
the Tigris River. Full of daring and a sense of adventure, they did
not feel like cutting wood before they had had some fun. "Let's
go across the river and explore the Kutterbul village," Hovsep
suggested.

"Yes," Toomas agreed, full of excitement. We've never seen the
little adobe village." The three cousins, Karnick, Kosrof, and
Serop, also agreed happily. They had always wanted to go there.
Now was the time for the adventure.

The boys hid their knives and ropes and turned to cross the
Tigris River, which was five hundred feet wide at this point but
fordable. Since not all of them could swim, they decided to wade
across, but Toomas, the shortest, found the water over his head.
"You ride on my back," said Hovsep. They all rolled their shirts
to their shoulders, took hold of each other's hands, and proceeded
across, Toomas on Hovsep's shoulders.

Toomas imagined that he was leading the way. "Hold tight,"
he cried to the others. "Follow me, I'm leading."

"My feet are slipping off the rocks," Serop yelled.

"Let's turn back," Kosrof pleaded.

Hovsep could not speak a word for Toomas's hands were
clasped tightly over his lips.

Toomas consoled them, "It won't be long now, boys. Just a
little more. Another step. Come on. Hold tight. Don't be a

coward!'' From his high perch he could afford to display courage, yet he trembled inwardly, wondering whether they would really make it. What if the current suddenly increased? What if they were carried away? There wouldn't be anyone to tell Mama!

Outwardly, he continued his encouragement. ''A few more steps and we'll be there.'' Still imagining, he assured them, ''The rocks are beginning to feel firmer under my feet. The water is now down to my waist. Didn't I tell you? There!''

At last, they found their feet on the other shore. They had conquered the Tigris! She was not invincible.

The boys removed their dripping clothes, spread them around to dry under the hot sun, and dropped their bodies gratefully on the ground. They lay motionless while the sun dried them off.

After they had rested awhile, they dressed and walked slowly and cautiously toward the village they had longed to see. But wait! Not a single soul advanced to meet them. No one came forward to greet them.

''Where are the people?'' Toomas asked. ''Why is everything so quiet?'' He looked in every direction.

''And where are the dogs?'' Hovsep wanted to know. A village without a chorus of howls and barks was not a village! And not one chimney sent up its smoke. There was not a soul astir, not a sign of motion. Even the air hung still like heavy fog.

''Look!'' Toomas cried, pointing a finger to an unhinged door. ''Let's see if there's anyone inside.'' The boys peeked through the window. Only the clear blue sky met their eyes. They checked another house whose door was missing completely. They found that house after house had walls and roof missing. The entire village was crumbling and had been deserted to decay by itself.

''What do you suppose happened to the people?'' Kosrof asked.

''I don't know, but let's get out of here,'' replied Hovsep.

''After all our trouble to cross the river,'' Serop complained.

''It's a ghost town!'' Karnick observed. ''Even the storks won't live here.'' Normally, there was not a single tower or elevated structure that was not crowned with nests of storks.

Not quite comprehending the mute testimony to the recent massacres, but full of disappointment, the boys hurried away from the dilapidated, empty village of Kutterbul. Overwhelmed with a sense of desolation, they returned to face the Tigris once more. For a time they had forgotten their plight in crossing, but now it all came back to them, and the river looked to them like a ravenous tiger.

But they could not retreat; they had conquered her once. Only how would they cross over *now*?

There were two ways to conquer this enemy. They could walk several miles to the only bridge, the Yeni Kopru. Or they could take the ferry boat, which was waiting at the shore.

Until that day, none of them had ever seen a boat. Awed by the wonder of this strange floating device, they remained speechless. What a marvelous, wonderful invention, this arrangement of crude lumber which could carry them across the river without getting their feet wet!

The boatman told them he would take them across for a fee. A fee? The boys looked at each other. No one had any money.

"What shall we do?" Karnick asked, with a worried look.

As usual, Toomas had the answer. "We'll tell him our story, how we are stranded and would he do us the favor?"

Hovsep shook his head. "It won't work. The boatman wants money."

After talking back and forth the boys came up with a plan. "He's an old man," Serop pointed out. "If he won't take us across voluntarily, we'll have to seize the "thing" and drive it ourselves."

"But we don't know how," Toomas argued. "Let's try saying nice things first." The boys decided to listen to Toomas.

Approaching the boatman, Karnick began, "Sir, you must be a very brave man, a superman, to drive that huge boat."

The old man studied the boys and smiled, "Well, it's not difficult for me." His dark eyes flashed with pleasure.

Toomas could not keep silent. "Sir, do you suppose you could still drive that boat with all of us on it? Would you have enough strength?"

The boatman gave a loud laugh. "You children don't know much about boats, do you?"

"Maybe all of our weight would be too much for you," Toomas persisted.

The man's eyes pierced Toomas's. "What are you driving at, son? Do you have the fee?" All the boys shook their heads.

The boatman spat into the water and squinted his eyes. Then he turned to them. "All right, boys, get into the boat and we'll see." Excitement raced through Toomas. He relished the thought of a new experience. What would it be like to conquer the giant Tigris in this "thing"?

Very cautiously, the boys stepped into the boat. Toomas

studied it carefully. It looked like a large rectangular mortar box.
Made of the most crude lumber, rough planking, could it
possibly be watertight? And with all their weight would the
"thing" sink? He stepped lightly for fear of falling through.

The boatman navigated with his long pole, with the expertise
of a master. The boys stood wide-eyed with wonderment. No one
said a word. No one moved. Spellbound, they watched the
boatman push the water of the mighty river behind them. It
seemed to take forever. Would this wooden box really make it to
the other side before the bottom fell out? Toomas dared not even
to breathe, lest the current of air rock the boat.

At last they reached land. Oh, the blessedness of the firm
ground beneath their feet! Never had the earth felt so solid to
Toomas and the others. They thanked the boatman with a pro-
fusion of compliments, with Toomas crying excitedly, "Oh, sir,
you are the bravest man I ever met! You must be the strongest
man in Kurdistan!"

The kind boatman accepted the flattering comments with great
pleasure and went back to his boat.

The day had been worthwhile, full of unexpected thrilling
adventure, but now the boys remembered they had come to the
banks of the Tigris for a purpose. They must get to work and cut
that wood!

Going straight to their cache, they unearthed the knives and
ropes they had hidden. With supercharged energy they went to
work, attacking the helpless trees, reenacting the bloody scenes
of the massacre back in Hini. Only this time, they, the Armenians, were the executioners!

They pretended their butcher knives were khandjars. With
fierce thrusts of the knives they hacked the trees left and right,
chopping off their heads and limbs with unabated vengeance—
their eyes blazing, their teeth gnashing, and their cries of retri-
bution filling the air. "There goes that Mohammedan's head!
Now his arm! Now his leg!"

Like the Kurds, they pretended to heed not to the shrills and
shrieks of the young and old, women and children, hacking
without discrimination, without mercy. The defenseless trees,
like a flock of gentle innocent lambs, did not protest. What good
would it have done them to protest?

Mercy did not exist. This was *their* day, as many days had been
for the cruel Kurds, they said. Only for them the day had been
short-lived. The sun had already gone down. Night was falling

fast. They must hurry or fall prey to the prowlers of the dark. Packing the bundles of freshly cut wood on their shoulders, they marched home with a triumphant song on their lips.

For this one day, this one short day, Toomas, his brother and three cousins had been conquerers. They had conquered the mighty Tigris, on foot and on planks, and they had played the executioner. A day to remember forever.

CHAPTER 23

Wonder of Wonders

Many months passed, while Pertoosh and her family tried to adjust to the pace of life in the city. Hini had become only a painful memory. The children—the boys—roamed the streets of Diyarbekir, fascinated by the sights and sounds. The main streets, unlike the up and down cobble streets of Hini, were leveled for coaches, carriages and wooden carts. The carts were driven by long-horned oxen, lumbering along at a snail's pace, but the coaches and carriages, drawn by horses who moved at lightning speed (it seemed to them), were something else. Hini was never like this!

Always seeking a thrill, Toomas, Hovsep, and their cousins often ran alongside the vehicles, begging the drivers to give them a ride. "Please, please, give us a ride," they would plead, running breathlessly for many blocks—all to no avail.

The drivers, from their elevated seats, could not see the boys, so sometimes they would hang on to the back of a carriage for a ride, which usually would not last long. Invariably, some bystander would see them and yell to the drivers, "Giaours riding on the back! Giaours riding on the back!"

Hearing this, the irate driver would crack his long whip backwards. The boys, laughing, would hold their grip until, after

94

many attempts, the whip struck their hands, stinging them. Sometimes the driver would snap his whip once or twice and thinking he was rid of the pesky boys, ride blissfully on. Should the driver stop suddenly on their account, they would run for their lives. Though riding a carriage illegally had its price, it was still a great deal of fun.

The new and strange wonders of the city never ceased to intrigue Toomas. One day as he wandered about, he noticed a large crowd of people milling around. Whatever it was they were congregating for, he had to see, too. He was drawn like a magnet. Somehow, he tunneled his way through the crowd, crawling where necessary through pairs of legs, no matter which sex.

What he saw filled him with amazement. Never had he seen anything like it. It was a wagon and yet not a wagon. It had four wheels, but unlike wagon wheels they were smaller and much thicker, with pretty carved designs over their round borders. They seemed to yield slightly at his touch. Perhaps that was due to the sun's heat, he thought, and decided it was a good thing that they had individual "shades" (fenders) over them.

The strange object had two compartments, both wide open on top, with a leather seat in each, like a sofa. In one compartment, set on a thick black rod, was a small wheel. That must be for a child to play with, Toomas told himself.

Now what was this thing? If it was a wagon, where was its tongue, or the futchel to hold the tongue between its jaws? Where was the elevated seat for the driver? Toomas scratched his head in great perplexity.

Presently, a man garbed in a general's uniform elbowed his way through the crowd, advancing toward the strange object. Without effort, he opened one side of a compartment. Toomas had not noticed the door, thinking one would have to climb over the sides to get into the thing.

The man sat in front of the small toy wheel, obviously waiting for a team of horses, thought Toomas. Suddenly, a noise like the sound of a dozen millstones grinding grain emitted from the thing. Surely the noise was not from the little toy wheel the man was playing with! Though he hung on to it, it was not moving at all.

All at once, the whole contraption, all by itself, moved a little. Toomas stepped back. Impossible! Filled with awe and wonderment, he stepped in front of it. Perhaps horses afar off were pulling with a rope. But there was no rope in sight.

Before he could find an answer, the object moved backwards. Incredible! Again he ran in front of it. Surely there had to be a rope, maybe an invisible one. But he would have stumbled over it! He stood there, dumbfounded, completely baffled.

All at once, an idea struck him. Perhaps the bottom of the compartment had an opening and the man's feet were pushing it. Why hadn't he thought of that before? To confirm his theory, he bent on hands and knees to look. No! That was not the answer.

I know, he told himself, some supernatural power, some weird spirit was moving it! While his mind was nearly bursting in astonishment, all at once, as though it had eyes to see, the bizarre object moved through the gaping, mystified crowd and disappeared.

No one had dared to touch it, fearing that a dangerous spirit might jump on him. Unable to unravel the mystery and crushed because he had not found an answer, Toomas went away. "A miracle. A miracle," he repeated to himself.

Shortly after he had witnessed this wonder, German soldiers began to pour into the city with similar vehicles and hundreds upon hundreds of other monstrous looking vehicles. Toomas learned that these were army trucks and that the first vehicle he had seen was an automobile! Marvelous inventions!

Before Toomas could solve the mystery of how the contraptions on wheels could run all by themselves, another, even more brain-boggling mystery appeared before him.

Full of boyish curiosity, he had gone to the barracks where the German soldiers lived. With Hovsep and his cousins, he went to see what German soldiers looked like and to hear their language. He remembered his cousin Benyamen, Pertoosh's sister's son. Before the massacre, he had been sent to Germany to study in the German ministry. Since the war, no one had heard from him. Had he been lost? Toomas recalled with pleasure how Benyamen used to entertain him for hours by juggling eggs. He was the best egg juggler in Hini.

The soldiers spoke an un-Asiatic language, strange to Toomas's ears. And they ate an odd-looking white something. One noon while a soldier was eating the strange food, Toomas kept staring hungrily until the soldier finally asked, "Want a piece?" Toomas nodded his head. "It's bread," the soldier said, answering the unspoken question—in Turkish.

"Bread? Why, our bread is always black," Toomas thought. He bit hungrily into the white, hard substance and savored his very first taste of white bread. It had a bland, pleasant taste and texture.

While looking around the barracks to see what they could see, the boys passed a barrack where a man was working under a tiny, funny-looking lamp—or was it a lantern? It hung suspended from the ceiling by a thick black cord. They watched the lamp go on and then off again, and Toomas suddenly realized that the man had not been near it. "Did you see that?" he asked the others. "The man wasn't even near that lamp when it went out and when it went on."

"Aw, we must be seeing things," Hovsep replied, with a puzzled look.

The boys had walked on a ways, but full of curiosity about the strange lamp, they decided to go back. They stood in the barrack's doorway and stared at the hanging lamp. A German soldier came to the door. "Haven't you ever seen an electric light before?" he asked. The boys looked dumbfounded. What was he talking about in his strange language?

"Here, I'll show you how it works." He went to the wall, pressed a small black button, and like magic, like lightning, the lamp lit up the room.

Toomas looked at Hovsep. Hovsep stared at Toomas. Were their eyes playing tricks? They had seen the heavy black cord running from the lamp to the small black button all right, but how could the soldier light the lamp through the long cord?

Toomas saw a box of matches on the bench. Had the soldier

used matches to light the lamp? He motioned to the matches. The soldier took the box of matches and placed them on the floor at his feet. Then he exposed his bare hands for their inspection. Next he went to the small black button and pressed it with one hand, and instantly, without a flicker, the lamp gave its bright light. Impossible! Why, the man had even turned his back to the lamp. He was not even looking at it! It was nothing short of a miracle!

They looked at the soldier, aghast. Who was this man who possessed such power? Full of bewilderment, the boys raced home, each wanting to be the first to tell their mother. They burst into the room, breathless, both of them talking and shouting at the same time, attempting to tell Pertoosh of the wonders they had seen that day.

CHAPTER 24

Hunger and Poisonous Weeds

When the cold snows of winter fell upon the city of Diyarbekir, the problem of finding wood to keep warm and food to sustain themselves became a major one for Pertoosh. The gold and silver coins had long since been spent for food. Most of the jewelry, through the efforts of the Effendi, had been traded for food and other necessities.

For weeks there had not been enough food to feed the children. Pertoosh's heart ached as she watched her children suffer from hunger. One evening she had served them a small dish of rice and given each one a piece of bread. With tears in his eyes, Toomas had cried, "Mama, may I have some more rice? I'm still hungry."

"Toomas, we have no more rice," she said sadly.

Toomas burst into tears. "But Hovsep has a bigger piece of bread than I."

Hovsep held his piece of bread tightly in his hand and shouted, "I do not!" Then he began to eat hungrily, even the morsels that fell.

Pertoosh wanted to cry. Her children, who had never before in their young lives known hunger, now used all the tricks and talk at their disposal to obtain a morsel of food. They went out of their way to be friendly with the Effendi's children, the ultimate motive being to get a bite of whatever they happened to be eating—and they were always munching on something.

The Effendi, aware of their need, had been most kind and had often sent food to them with Zaabel. But Pertoosh recognized that even his kindness would have limits. She did not wish to become a burden to him.

With the passing days, the children's hunger increased. One morning the Effendi's son stood in the courtyard eating a large piece of bread. Toomas stood nearby, watching with the agony of hunger. When the boy raised the tantalizing bread to his mouth, Toomas went through the same motion. When the boy began to masticate, Toomas moved his mouth, pretending that he, too, was savoring the precious food. Oh, the agony to his salivating taste buds, his growling stomach!

Pertoosh's heart filled with anguish as she watched Toomas and as she pondered the events of the past. How she missed Garabed. How she wished he were by her side to comfort and provide for their children. The massacre had reduced them from millionaires to paupers! She could not help thinking of the days of abundance, of joy and health. How blessed they had been!

Her thoughts came back to face the reality of the moment. What could she do to provide food for her children? Surely there had to be a way. She opened the large Bible they had brought with them and read to the children, "Consider the ravens: for they neither sow nor reap; which neither have storehouse nor barn; and God feedeth them: how much more are ye better than the fowls?" (Luke 12:24)

A few days later an idea came to her. She remembered that the Effendi supervised a Turkish orphanage for older boys. Perhaps if she went to him and asked, he would be willing to place Hovsep in the orphanage. He would have plenty to eat and she would have one less mouth to feed.

Full of apologies and humility, she approached their benefactor. "Effendi," she began, "you have been very kind to us, and we are very grateful. I would ask one more favor of you."

"Yes, Pertoosh?" he replied kindly.

"Would you take my son Hovsep and place him in your Turkish orphanage?"

The Effendi remained silent for one long moment. What was he thinking, Pertoosh wondered. Was she, at last, asking too much from this kind man who had taken them in and cared for them?

At last he spoke. "Pertoosh, there is a problem, you know. Hovsep is not Turkish."

Pertoosh felt her heart sink. "Yes, that is true."

"But wait, Pertoosh," he smiled. "If Hovsep will not reveal his nationality, I will have him admitted."

Pertoosh breathlessly answered, "Oh, but of course. He will never reveal his nationality," she promised.

"One more thing," the Effendi said in a solemn tone. "Hovsep must never say he is related to me by marriage."

Pertoosh smiled under her veil. "Yes, Effendi. I can promise he will never reveal our relationship."

"All right. You may take him to the orphanage within a couple of days. I will arrange things."

Pertoosh, holding back tears, could not thank him enough.

A few months later, Pertoosh learned of the need for a cook at the orphanage and applied for the job. But the Effendi protested, "No, no, Pertoosh. This cannot be. What will people say if they learn my wife's aunt is working here? It will be a disgrace for me."

Desperate in her need, Pertoosh persisted. "But Effendi, times have changed. Now there is a great deal of hardship and starvation."

A day passed, and the Effendi came to her with a suggestion. Pertoosh brightened when she saw him. "Pertoosh, I have been giving this matter a great deal of thought. I know your need and I want to help you." His kind eyes were filled with sympathy.

"Effendi, we will do anything you say," Pertoosh assured him.

"You know, of course, that it would be a great embarrassment to my position if you were seen coming home from the orphanage to my house each night, do you not?"

"Yes, I understand."

"If you and your family were to move away, then if you worked at the orphanage, no one would see you coming here," the Effendi said.

"Do you mean I may have the job at the orphanage if we move away from here?"

"Yes, Pertoosh. You may have the job, if you will find other living quarters," the Effendi said kindly.

Pertoosh did not hesitate. Sixteen people in one room had become unbearable. "Oh, but of course. We will be happy to do as you say."

Shortly afterwards, Pertoosh found a small house with very low rent and moved her family, which now consisted of Toomas, Victoria and herself. The rest of the family, aunts and cousins, were compelled to move also and found themselves a house in a nearby village. So the families parted, each to survive on its own.

Pertoosh became head cook at the orphanage. But her meager wages were hardly enough to pay the rent for their two shanty rooms. While she could eat her meals at the orphanage, she need-ed food for Toomas and Victoria.

Again she turned to the Effendi. "Master," she pleaded, "I have no money with which to buy food for my children. How can I eat and watch my children starve?"

"Oh, no, Pertoosh. We must do something. Have Toomas come to the orphanage to eat, but do not let anyone know," the Effendi replied.

"And Victoria?" Pertoosh persisted. "May I take food home to her at night?"

"Yes, but do not let anyone see you," the Effendi warned. Once again, Pertoosh expressed her profound thanks to this man who had saved them from starvation.

As wonderful as the arrangement sounded, however, it was easier said than done. At his first opportunity, Toomas walked casually to the back gate of the orphanage. Now how could he get into the kitchen without being observed? Some of the workers knew he was the son of the cook, but no one must know he was the brother of *ooch-use-otooz-dokooz nombralli Yousooff* (Hovsep's number and name).

Furtively, he looked around. When he was sure no one had seen him, he dashed into the kitchen. When Mama saw him, she whispered, "Toomas, quick, get into this little room. Stay here and I will bring you food."

Toomas hid himself in the small dark room behind the kitchen. He waited, sitting on the bare ground, while his stomach growled with hunger. Would Mama never come? He was so hungry he would be able to eat a whole lamb, he told himself. It seemed an eternity before she came.

At last, the door creaked open slowly. Pertoosh handed him a large object. "Mama, what is it?" Toomas asked in the dark.

"It's a lamb's head. Eat it and be quiet," Pertoosh said and closed the door behind her.

Alone with the lamb's head, Toomas worked hurriedly and guardedly. No one must find him and take it away. He wrestled with it until he cracked the skull. On his knees, sometimes squatting, sometimes kneeling, he attacked the lamb's head. He ate like a ravenous wolf, full of fervor and excitement, deftly spooning the savory brain with trained fingers. The aroma tantalized his nostrils, and his tongue savored every delightful mouthful.

Neither the caviar of the generals nor the ambrosia of the gods could, for Toomas, have surpassed this delectable feast. Only two heads, instead of one, could have brought more delight.

One thing marred the privilege of eating at the orphanage. Toomas was unable to go through the gate undetected every day, succeeding only three or four times a week. The rest of the days he would wait with Victoria till late at night, when Pertoosh came home with her little lunch pail. Toomas sat up for hours, waiting and trying to appease his ravaged stomach. How impatiently he waited to see Pertoosh as she entered the door with her round pail hidden under her voluminous skirt, and how quickly he reached for it. Victoria, just as hungry as he, would always have to grab the pail and remind him to save some for her.

Mama Pertoosh, working from fourteen to sixteen hours every day, came home exhausted. She walked the dark narrow winding streets, full of mud and mire, in the bitter cold and strong wind. Sometimes she waded through small streams over jagged, flesh-tearing rocks, with her shoes in her hands. Always she carried food for her starving children at home. Often, soaked to the skin, her cheeks wet with tears of fatigue, her feet swollen, bleeding and aching, she would fall weakly into Victoria's restful arms.

The meager portions of bread and whatever else Pertoosh could smuggle out of the kitchen were not, however, sufficient for Toomas and Victoria. Occasionally they went outside the walls of the city to pick different kinds of greens and grass. One evening Pertoosh boiled a variety of greens resembling lamb's quarters.

She placed it before the children and invited them to eat.

"No," said Toomas, even though he was starving. He held his empty stomach, crying, "I don't like the smell of it!" But Pertoosh and Victoria, full of hunger, ate all they could hold.

Around midnight, Toomas heard Victoria's cry of distress, "Help me. Mama, Mama, I am—terribly sick." Instantly, Toomas ran to her side. Pertoosh tried to lift herself from her bed, but fell back in pain.

Panic stricken, Toomas cried, "Mama, what is wrong with you and Victoria?" He knelt beside her.

"I—I'm—too dizzy to get up," Pertoosh's voice was filled with pain. "Oh—my—stomach."

As Pertoosh lay back on her bed, she fell into a delirium, calling over and over, "Garabed, Garabed."

"What shall I do? Mama, Mama—talk to me!" Toomas placed an arm around his mother. He heard Victoria heaving and ran to help her. Pains wracked her body and twisted her face.

A faint cry came from Pertoosh. "Toomas—go—go—next door—to our neighbor and get—some—*madzoon* (yogurt).

Instantly, Toomas was at the door. "Yes, Mama. I'll hurry back." Within a few minutes he returned with the madzoon. Kneeling on the floor beside his mother, he spooned it into her mouth. Then he went to Victoria and fed it to her.

Pertoosh and Victoria recovered in a few hours.

"Mama," Toomas said thoughtfully the next day, "Those were not lamb's quarters; they were a poisonous weed! I'm glad I didn't eat any."

"You were smart, Toomas. And without the madzoon, we might have died," Pertoosh said gratefully.

"I'm glad you knew the remedy for weed poisoning," Toomas told Pertoosh. He loved his mother.

Then he added, "Mama, I want to be a doctor when I grow up. I want to go to America, and be a doctor there. Do you think we will ever go?"

"If God wills, we will go," Pertoosh replied with a prayer in her heart. More than anything in the world now she wanted to take her children and go to America. America—the word was synonymous with heaven.

While Pertoosh struggled to keep her family alive, Hovsep, now called by the Turkish name of Yousooff, had adapted very well at the orphanage. Too well, Pertoosh thought. Her son, by absorbing Turkish culture and mores, by his close friendships with Turkish boys, had gradually alienated himself from his Armenian heritage.

Pertoosh worried and prayed, "Lord, let my son not forget the faith of his father. And not forget that Garabed yielded his life for Christianity."

Several months later, Pertoosh learned that all the boys of Hovsep's age at the orphanage would be sent via army trucks to Istanbul. From there they would be sent to Germany for an education and special training for the Turkish government.

She went at once to her son. "Hovsep, you do not need to go to Germany. I will speak to the Effendi to exempt you."

Hovsep stared at his mother with an incredulous expression. "But, Mama," he cried, "I *want* to go. It is the best thing that could happen to me. I will have a future!"

"A future as a Turkish son?" Pertoosh asked.

Hovsep turned away. "I'm *going*, Mama. *Nothing* can change my mind."

With a heavy heart, Pertoosh admitted to herself that her son could not be dissuaded. Toomas, listening to the conversation, piped up, "You are going to ride in an army truck, aren't you?"

Hovsep's eyes lighted up. "Yes! All the way to Istanbul!"

"I wish I were going, too!" Toomas's voice was choked with envy.

Pertoosh saw the fascination the army trucks held for the boys and knew they would give anything for even a mere ride in one of them. It was useless to talk to Hovsep to try to change his mind. It was like talking to the wall.

Having failed in her efforts, she began to advise him. "Hovsep, hold fast. Do not forget you are a Christian."

"I won't," Hovsep answered lightly.

"When you arrive in Istanbul, write to your brother Aghegsanter. Tell him where you are. Tell him about us. Maybe he will send for you to go to America," Pertoosh instructed.

"All right, Mama. I promise." He kissed his mother, brother, and sister goodbye, and shortly afterward, laughing and singing with the Turkish boys in the army truck, he departed for Istanbul.

Pertoosh watched the truck until it vanished into the distance. Hovsep had blended with the Turkish boys. No one would suspect his Armenian parentage. Would he forget his racial ties, his mother tongue, his family? Her tears flowed silently and she prayed that God would watch over her son and that someday she would see him again.

CHAPTER 25

Starvation Strikes

Shortly after Hovsep left for Istanbul, Pertoosh lost her job at the orphanage. With all the young men leaving for training, her services as a cook were no longer required. The Effendi showed great regret, but Pertoosh felt that her world, formerly secured by her job, had finally come crashing down upon her.

Hovsep had been the "man of the family" because he was the eldest male. Now feelings of utter loneliness haunted Pertoosh. Even Victoria and Toomas felt the emptiness created by Hovsep's absence.

With misty eyes Pertoosh said to Toomas, "Now you are the 'man of the family.'"

"Mama, I'm *eight* years old." He stood up straight, full of pride because now he was the "man of the family." Yet what could he do to bring food to his mother and sister, when thousands of orphans, hungry and homeless, roamed the streets?

The massacre of the Armenians by the Turks had taken place in Diyarbekir at the same time as in Hini and every other city and village where Armenians lived. Unity of time had assured their success, for the Armenian populace, caught by surprise, was unable to flee, resist or retaliate.

Now the streets were filled with women and children and a few men, who by some miracle had escaped the slaughter. They wandered in the streets scantily clad, some with only a dirty rag around their waists. Since they were homeless, they could not escape the ravages of the bitter cold day and night.

Some, having lost their last ounce of strength, lay prostrate in the streets, unable to move, waiting for death to end their misery. Others, wounded and sick, walked around the market places, looking for a grain of wheat that might have fallen. Many ate whatever they could find in the heaps of rubbish. Others were too feeble to eat, and could not have swallowed food even if it had been offered them.

All of the neighborhoods were plagued with beggars. Like watchmen they guarded the gates of houses, their eyes glued to the latch. If a door latch clicked somewhere, dozens of beggars came running from all directions with outstretched hands and gaping mouths.

Some sat stationed by the gate of their former home, begging from new and calloused occupants, and refused to move. Sometimes, instead of alms, they received merciless beatings, but still they begged with tears and supplications. Each one had his own peculiar chant, and their whining tones filled the air day and night.

Toomas, who walked the streets often, was filled with compassion at the sight of these ragged, starved, emaciated creatures, who had once been normal human beings. Their cries and unbearable echoes always rang in his ears long after he reached home.

The saddest were the little children, with their torn ragged clothing hanging loosely from their thin, bony shoulders, their hair gnarled, faces unwashed, eyes mattered, feet bare and bleeding from open sores. *"Mammy, Astoozo seeroon!"* they cried. *"Mammy, baadar mu hatz, mammy! Mammy, hadjees, mammy, Astoozo seeroon!"* ("Mammy, for God's sake, Mammy, a morsel of bread, mammy! Mammy, please, mammy, for God's sake!") These tiny bits of humanity—mere skeletons—roamed the streets in search of bread and shelter.

And no one seemed to care.

Toomas counted his blessings. Though they were often hungry, they still had bread. Pertoosh and Victoria devised ways to eke out a meager livelihood, and they had help from Pesa, a young Armenian who had escaped the massacre by enlisting in the Turkish army. He had fallen in love with Victoria and was courting her. Toomas was very fond of him.

With Pesa's help, the women bought cotton and knit stockings or spun thread from it. Sometimes they sewed fancy quilted jackets for army officers. They made tufted bed quilts for Turkish *hannums* (ladies). And they spent many hours crocheting doilies and making delicate embroidered articles which they exchanged with Turkish ladies for food.

Countless times, when they had only a piece of bread to eat, Pertoosh said to Victoria and Toomas, "We must be grateful for this piece of bread, and thank God that we have it."

Toomas knew that many times his mother had gone hungry because she had saved her bread for him. It was not the plain dark bread they had been accustomed to, but black, muddy tasting, indigestible, full of straws two and three inches long, and dipped in ashes to mask its flavor.

And many times Toomas, in turn, had saved his morsel of bread to share with the starving children outside their door. Taking the piece of bread to his mouth he would say, "See, Mama, instead of this going into my stomach," and then would jerk it out of his mouth and walk to the window and drop it down into an ever-open hand.

Pertoosh, overwhelmed by what he did, often took him in her arms and showered him with kisses, crying, "Toomas, my precious one. God will bless you for this." The feel of her wet cheek against his own was all the reward Toomas wanted, and inspired him to repeat his act of mercy.

Sometimes Pertoosh would take in the starving orphans, give them a blanket and let them sleep in the sheltered courtyard. These children were infested with fleas that somehow filled the house. Afraid of the possibility of some terrible disease, Pertoosh spent a great deal of time cleaning the house and boiling the blankets. She could not forget the costly price of taking in the little orphan girl who had been so sick with cholera in Hini.

Every day Turkish soldiers came with their oxen-driven wagons to pick up the dead in the streets and take them to the Tigris River where they dumped the bodies. They did not confine their "pick-up" assignment to just the dead. Sometimes the half-dead, with screeches of pain, dragged themselves along the walls of buildings to escape the fate of being picked up and dumped into the river. Some cried, "No, no!" when the soldiers dragged them to the wagons. The soldiers said to each other, "Less work for tomorrow, if the half-living are picked up with the dead."

Toomas cringed when he saw the wagons rumbling over the cobblestone streets at a fast pace, knowing that among the dead were some who breathed and squirmed. The wagons headed for Leron Toor, one of the four gates of Diyarbekir, and from there to the river, to dump the living and the dead into their watery graves. These cargoes were human—people once loved and cared for. How could it be? Toomas agonized within himself.

On one of his walks in the streets among the starving masses, Toomas saw someone he thought he recognized, a young man with a blank, cadaverous look. Covered only with a shredded rag, he presented a pitiful picture. Toomas squinted his eyes and tried to remember. He was sure he knew the young man. Who was he?

Suddenly, like a flash of lightning, he knew. That figure, that shadow, was his cousin Nishon! They had grown up together. They had played together right here in Diyarbekir, but when the family parted they lost touch with each other.

The bright beautiful eyes that Toomas remembered were now pale gray, almost colorless. The rosy red cheeks had become like parchment stretched over protruding bones. What had been blond wavy hair lay snarled, full of sand and straw, like a bird's nest. The young body, once strong and robust, now showed embossed countable ribs. With thin, almost fleshless arms, swollen abdomen, and legs that looked like stilts, Nishon was a mere skeleton. The blithe spirit he had always possessed had been replaced with a haunted melancholy expression.

Toomas couldn't believe his eyes. He stood, transfixed, staring at the walking ghost. Collecting himself, he called, "Nishon, Nishon!" But his calls fell on deaf ears. Nishon, walking as though in a trance, seemed to be carried, without resistance, by a gust of wind. Toomas kept calling and pushing through the crowds. But Nishon, totally insensate to his cries, vanished into the masses.

Crushed and heartsick, Toomas went home and told Pertoosh. Pertoosh wept. "Do you think you can find him, Toomas?" she asked.

"I'm going to try," Toomas replied with tears in his eyes. "Mama, he was skin and bones. It didn't even look like him."

The following day, with a piece of black bread in his pocket, Toomas went searching for his cousin. He pushed and shoved his way through the beggars and starvelings, but Nishon was nowhere to be seen. He made many inquiries and learned, finally, that the boy had been picked up with several others the previous afternoon, by the death-wagon.

Full of sorrow and regrets, Toomas told himself he would never, till he drew his last breath, forget the haunted look on his cousin's face. "Why does there have to be so much starvation?" he cried to his mother.

CHAPTER 26

The Enterprising Young Merchant

The bitter cold of winter gave way to the spring sunshine of 1917. As blossoms sprang forth from the earth and the trees put on their mantle of green, the time came when Pertoosh realized she could no longer afford to remain in the little rented house. After searching, she managed to rent an inexpensive room directly across from a Turkish hospital where Victoria's suitor, Pesa, worked as an attendant. From their rooms, within speaking distance, they carried on a courtship.

Pertoosh grew fond of the young man. Only she, Victoria, and Toomas knew his secret—that he was not Turkish, but Armenian—and kept it sacredly.

Pesa's friendship continued to help save them from hunger. Sometimes, taking Toomas to market with him, he would say, "Take this fruit [or whatever he had purchased] to Victoria." Toomas obliged happily, for of course Victoria always shared her food.

109

Later, as the romance blossomed, when Pesa came to visit Victoria he always brought a loaf of bread tucked under his army overcoat. Handing it to her, he would say with a smile, "For you and your family, Victoria." The muddy black bread seemed like manna from heaven. A bouquet of flowers for Victoria could not have been more welcome.

Sometimes Pesa said to Toomas, "Tonight come to the back door of the hospital kitchen and I will give you a package." The package always proved to be a loaf of bread.

In spite of her fondness for Pesa, Pertoosh would not allow him to visit Victoria unless she or Toomas were there to chaperone. Toomas felt important indeed, to have such a duty at his young age.

Toomas felt strongly all the responsibilities of being the "man of the family." He asked himself what could he, a nine-year-old do? He had not one *monkur* (penny) to his name. Perhaps if he walked about town he would get some ideas.

With this in mind, he started out one morning and had gone only a few blocks when a soldier flipped away a half-smoked cigarette. At once, a bright idea flashed into Toomas's mind. That unsmoked cigarette half was just as good as the smoked half!

Without any hesitation, he gave himself the job of going about the streets picking up half-smoked cigarettes. Within a few hours his pockets and shirt-tail bulged with cigarette stubs.

These are worth a fortune, he told himself. Bursting with satisfaction, he went home to treat and prepare them for resale. When Pertoosh saw the bulges, she asked, "What have you there?"

"Mama, remember how we used to make Dada Khazzar's cigarettes for him?"

"Yes." Pertoosh looked surprised.

"Well, I'm going to make new cigarettes from these and sell them. You'll see." He emptied his pockets and shirt-tail into a pan. Pertoosh smiled with a great deal of pleasure.

Toomas sprayed the tobacco with a little water to make it soft and fluffy and pliable—field fresh. Pertoosh asked her little man, "What will you do for cigarette papers?"

"I'll sell a few batches in bags first. Then I'll buy a book of cigarette papers."

Toomas's first business enterprise met with success at once. He bought the cigarette papers and rolled the cigarettes daily, then sold them one by one.

There arose a demand for matches to light the cigarettes. He could not supply his customers with free matches, nor could he charge them the same price he paid in the retail stores. Wracking his brain, he came up with a solution. He bought matches, took them home and emptied the boxes. Next, he placed a thick piece of cardboard on the bottom of the boxes and refilled them loosely. Now two boxes yielded three.

As the days passed, although Toomas was happy to hand over to Pertoosh the few monkurs he earned, he found the total profit for a day's labor not to his satisfaction. He must find a way to make more money.

Possibly, he told himself, he could make more money by peddling boiled acorns. It was absolutely taboo for a woman to smoke cigarettes, but everyone, including women, ate acorns, so he would have more customers.

He began by buying a panful of acorns and selling them by the dozen. Then he learned that they would cost less if purchased in larger quantity. He asked Pertoosh, "Mama, will you let me buy a hundred-pound sack, so I will make more money?"

Pertoosh agreed to let him use his hard-earned monkurs to purchase a sackful. Victoria volunteered to help, saying, "I'll boil them for you, and Mama can go with you to the market to watch over the sack while you sell them."

"Yes," Pertoosh agreed. "You would not be able to keep the poor beggars from snatching your sack from you." She went with Toomas, and while he made the sales, she sat by the sack and guarded it.

Before long the market became flooded with acorns. It seemed that everybody was selling them, and Toomas had to look for something else to peddle.

A new idea came to him one day when they were having meat— a rare treat—for dinner. Why not make small meatballs and sell them? He was sure no one had ever thought of *that* before, for meat, in any form, was not sold in the streets.

"May I, Mama? Please, will you and Victoria make the small meatballs?" His eyes searched his mother's for approval.

At first Pertoosh hesitated, then she said, "I'm not really sure they will sell, but we must do something to earn money. We'll try it."

Toomas circled his arms around her waist and cried, "Oh, Mama, I want so much to earn money to take care of you and Victoria."

"You're a good boy, Toomas, and a very good businessman." She laughed.

"Some day, when we go to America, I'll make *lots* of money for you. You'll see. They say there is gold to be had just for the taking. Can you imagine that, Mama?"

"If it is God's will, some day we will go to America," Pertoosh replied. At the moment, it seemed like an impossible dream.

Pertoosh and Victoria made the meatballs and Toomas introduced them at the market. "Meatballs! Meatballs! Eat your meatballs while they're hot! Everybody!" Toomas called at the top of his voice.

People stopped and smiled and bought the tasty meatballs. Before long, Toomas had sold all he had. Full of excitement and happiness, he ran home to report to Pertoosh. "Mama, I sold out in the first hour!"

"We'll make more," Pertoosh said with wonderment.

But an unforeseen problem arose. Toomas discovered that there was a scarcity of meat and that the price had skyrocketed. He could not afford to pay the price, and his new venture vanished into thin air. His brief taste of success left him full of disappointment, but in spite of it he would not cease to be a businessman. He had to come up with a new idea. He was sure he had an inexhaustible supply. What could he do next?

Walking around the market place searching for a new idea, he observed that the madzoon was sold in oaken buckets of different sizes. He reasoned that it must be in great demand, and that if the demand for large quantities was great, would not the demand for small quantities, individual helpings, be just as great? Why not have Mama and Victoria make the madzoon at home, and he could sell it by the cup?

Pertoosh agreed to make the madzoon, and Toomas took a panful to the market. Those who sold it by the bucket sat in one place until sold out, but sitting was not for Toomas. Instead of waiting for people to come to him, he approached them, with his pan of madzoon in one hand and a tin cup in the other. Going from one street to the other, and striking the cup against the pan to catch attention, he yelled, *"Yogurt! Dotlee durr boo yogurt!"* ("Sweet yogurt!")

When a customer came by, he dipped the cup into the pan and handed it to him. The customer drank it and handed back the cup. Toomas then refilled the same cup and sold its contents to another customer.

After a few days, Toomas found his profit from yogurt sales was not enough to sustain the family. Coming up with another idea, he said to Pertoosh, "Mama, it seems my customers have a hard time swallowing the thick yogurt. Why not dilute it with water for their benefit?"

Pertoosh laughed. "You are indeed a shrewd business man! But if you dilute it, you will have *taan* [buttermilk]."

"Then I will sell them taan! That would double or triple my profits!" Toomas could hardly contain himself for his clever idea.

As his profits grew and he became more experienced, he added more water to the yogurt. Since the profit lay in the dilution, he kept adding water to the yogurt, being careful to preserve its white color, the color being his gauge. The dilution, of course, yielded a greatly watered taan, but then, since he was his own boss, he could do as he pleased! Besides, wasn't he doing it for the customer's benefit, so he could swallow it more easily?

Now, instead of yelling "Yogurt!" he covered the streets yelling "*i-ron!*" (another name for taan). His business brought in incredible profit, as there was hardly any overhead. But, somehow, good things didn't seem to last for Toomas.

Within a short time, as the dilution rate went up, customer sales went down, and Toomas soon found himself without customers for his watered-down i-ron. Did his customers think they had been victimized? Wasn't he at least to be commended for replenishing their daily quota of water?

Now he had to think of another way to make money!

It seemed that Pertoosh and Victoria were always in need of buttons for the garments they made to sell, and in these trying times they could not afford to buy any. Since Toomas was the "man of the house" he felt the responsibility of finding a way to obtain the buttons. Once again, he put his ingenuity to work.

All about the city were the *yengee doonias*. These were a kind of rectangular wooden box arrangement where people gathered to see "movies." The boxes sat on legs painted in kaleidoscopic colors with two or three set of small holes in front for viewing.

On top of the "magic" boxes were two miniature cupolas with an opening in the back large enough for the operator to insert his hands. Inside was a scroll of pictures fastened on a parchment which rolled and unrolled on one stick at each end. The owner-operator stood behind, holding the sticks and rotating the scroll for the viewer. As the pictures came into view, he described them to the viewer.

The customers sat on a wooden stool or bent down in front of the modern marvels and looked through the twin holes. A small candle illuminated the darkness.

For his viewing pleasure, the enthralled customer paid one to five monkurs, depending on the elaborateness of the yengee doonia. The amount of business depended on the operator's persuasiveness and humor to make the pictures sensational and truly life-like.

After studying several of these "movie houses" Toomas decided to make his own. His customers were mostly children. Since buttons were easier to obtain than monkurs from the children, soon he had an abundance of buttons—all sizes and colors—for his mother and sister.

His ingenuity did not stop there. On one of his days off, Pertoosh asked him to make an extra set of knitting needles. Toomas knew that his mother was proud of his ability to make things, and would never ask him to make anything unless she was sure he could. She showed her pride in his ability by wearing the knolleens he had made since Hovsep had gone away.

Pertoosh's knitting needles were made of celluloid. What could Toomas use to make a new pair? He searched for an answer. On an early-morning jaunt around the walls of the city, he came upon a cast-off broken umbrella. His eyes fell on the strips of steel fastened to the center rod. He picked it up and ran his fingers over the steel. It had the same elasticity as the celluloid needles! Why not use it to make new knitting needles?

With Pertoosh's approval, he made a set. To prove they were as workable as the celluloid kind, he knit a pair of stockings with them. Then an idea exploded in his mind—why not make knitting needles to sell?

He began collecting broken, useless umbrellas and making needles. He worked enthusiastically because the proceeds were one hundred percent profit. They sold as fast as he could make them. In his mind he saw himself someday constructing a large factory and hiring and training employees to manufacture knitting needles.

He had sold many sets when he realized that he was making the needles of such durable material that they would last the owner a lifetime, unlike the celluloid kind which broke easily and would burn. It was not long before he ran out of customers and found himself with several surplus sets on his hands. Out of business once again!

By now Toomas had made many friends among the business people. His enterprising ways had attracted several storekeepers. One *khankeeper* (innkeeper), Hamid, took a liking to him. Toomas ran errands occasionally for Hamid, and it occurred to him that Hamid might give him a job if he should ask for it. Conflicting thoughts churned around in his mind. A part of him said, "No, you're too independent to work for someone else. Be your own businessman," and "Besides, he may turn you down. Don't you have any pride?" But another part of him realized that he needed to earn money for his family. Wasn't he the man of the family? He decided on a plan that might induce Hamid to offer him a job, without his having to ask for it.

Early every morning he went to the khan and voluntarily swept the floors, brushed the cobwebs off the walls, and made himself useful. Hamid seemed very pleased to see him doing chores without being asked. One morning when Toomas appeared with the first rays of the sun, Hamid smiled and said, "Toomas, how would you like a job?"

"A job? Doing what, Hamid?" Toomas pretended slight indifference. He mustn't seem too eager.

"You can start by taking my lodgers' animals to water."

"I'd like that," Toomas tried to keep the excitement out of his voice. "When do I start?"

"Right now."

Hamid's khan was about half a mile from Aslan-Kaplan, a fountain that spurted water from the mouths of two large statues of lions. Nearby, at Nor Toor, were the government buildings.

Toomas felt a stream of pride rush through his veins. The fountain was open to the public, and anyone could go to drink or carry water. But *he* would be privileged. How many would go there on horseback in times like these? He would look like a prince on his steed.

He learned that Hamid's khan did an exclusive business, boarding some of the finest Arabian horses in Kurdistan. These horses belonged to army officers and cheiftains. Sometimes Hamid catered to camels, mules and donkeys.

Toomas's duties also included taking stallion horses to other khans for breeding purposes. While he enjoyed the work, he found working with the stallions very trying as they were difficult to manage. Still, he enjoyed his job. He was doing fun work and getting paid for it! For the first time in his life, he was getting regular pay for his services. Would wonders never cease?

While riding the horses to water, Toomas rode bareback—no saddle for him! He preferred the spirited horses that strutted and pranced. The way he rode them, bystanders would think he owned not only the prancing horse, but the entire world! That is, until one day he had an experience that he would remember the rest of his life.

That morning Hamid asked, "We have a horse here that is unbroken. Do you think you can manage him?"

Coming from his boss, the question was an affront to Toomas's valor—and a challenge. "Sure, Hamid," he replied. "I can ride *any* horse."

"But this one is wild and incorrigible."

"Just try me." Toomas pulled himself to full height. He knew Hamid took pride in his daring ways, his seeming lack of fear. He would show him.

He rode the beautiful stallion to Aslan-Kaplan without any problems. What did Hamid mean, he was wild? Why, he was so tame it was a little boring. After the horse drank his fill, Toomas decided to show him who was in command. He would show Hamid that he was a born cavalier, not just an ignorant stable boy.

He picked up a small twig from the ground, then drew the horse alongside an embankment so he could mount him. Slowly, carefully, lest the horse show an evil intention, he slid over his back. Hardly had he straddled him when he touched his behind with the twig. Instantly the stallion reacted, as though he were taking off on a magic carpet.

The horse reared upward in the air, like a dog reaching for a bone held high over its reach. Luckily for Toomas, the horse's hind hooves had sunk into the mud, holding him there securely. Who knows where Toomas might have landed otherwise? For a moment, he hung on the horse for his very life. It seemed an eternity before the front hooves landed on the ground.

Toomas had thought this horse was tame? Why, he had turned out to be a highbred courser, a Shakespearean "hot and fiery steed." Had there been fire or whiskey or something in the water he drank?

Suddenly, after the frenzied animal had bucked and leaped a

few more times, he took off like lightning, like a champion sprinter, luckily toward the khan. Was he going sixty, seventy, eighty, maybe ninety miles per second? It seemed to Toomas the speed of lightning. Fear gripped him, and he dropped the reins. He tried to reach for them, but they eluded his grasp. Seeing his danger, he became horrified. He grasped the horse's mane with a death grip, hoping his weight would not pull it out. Now as the horse leaped through the air, Toomas found himself seesawing from one side of the horse's ribs to the other, as though riding on air.

The horse continued his mad pace through the streets while bystanders fled left and right out of his path. Some, trying to be helpful, held a cane before him. Others threw rags or burlap sacks in his path, not realizing they were stoking an uncontrollable fire.

The horse had just about reached the khan when Hamid, who seemed to be waiting for them, darted into the street. What was he going to do—exhibit his heroism by trying to stop the frantic animal?

Suddenly the fear left Toomas, like a robe slipping to the ground. Hamid would rescue him.

Hamid made one long leap and his Herculean arms encircled the horse's neck. His massive weight followed like an anchor, and the horse, taken by surprise, came to a miraculous halt. Instantly, Toomas leaped to the ground, which moved beneath his feet for several minutes.

When Hamid had tied the horse, he came to Toomas. "You look like a ghost, Toomas, but I'm proud of you. You stayed on the horse. That takes a lot of skill, boy." Toomas smiled weakly. He felt his legs wobble beneath him. If Hamid only knew!

After this experience with an untamed horse, Toomas found that somehow fear of horses no longer existed for him. He became as calloused as the foreknees of a camel.

CHAPTER 27

Robbed and Beaten

Many months passed while Pertoosh, with Victoria and Toomas's help, struggled to survive in the midst of widespread
starvation. When the opportunity came to sub-rent a rear room
from an Armenian couple for a small sum, Pertoosh took it.
Although entrance and exit could only be gained by passing
through the couple's living quarters, Pertoosh was happy for the
room.

The couple were Gigo, who was in his mid-thirties, and his
wife, Rozo. Shortly after Pertoosh and her family had moved into
their new room, Toomas asked, "Mama, how is it that Gigo was
not massacred like Papa?"

"I do not know, Toomas, but you must not ask such questions." Pertoosh dropped her knitting needles and searched his
face.

"But, Mama, doesn't it seem strange that he was not khand-
jared like the rest of our men?" Toomas persisted, with resentment in his voice.

Victoria added her observation, "I'm wondering how Rozo is
able to dress so well. They seem to be living in luxury when all
around us people are starving."

"They don't have any children," Toomas added. "Why can't
they help those who are starving?"

They had many questions about their new neighbors, but no
answers.

Through their association they learned that Gigo had much
experience in business dealings and knowledge of world affairs.
And he knew his way around the city. A bright idea came to
Toomas. He went to Pertoosh and rationalized, "Mama, do you
agree that I have had lots of experience as a peddler?"

Pertoosh laughed. "Yes, I would say you have learned a great
deal about the business world."

"Then, Mama, do you think Gigo would help me start a small business?"

Pertoosh looked up from her sewing. "What kind of business, Toomas?" She did not seemed surprised at his question.

"A small confectionery store?" Toomas's voice rose with excitement. "I could quit my job at the khan and make lots more money as a merchant." Lately he had often dreamed of becoming a merchant, but there was one big obstacle. He would need "capital" to start a business.

To his surprise, Pertoosh came to the rescue. "I think your idea is a good one. I have one piece of gold sovereign hidden for an emergency. You may use it to buy your merchandise."

Toomas jumped up and down and kissed his mother. "Thank you, thank you, Mama. I'll be successful, you'll see. I'll make lots of money for you."

One evening soon afterwards Pertoosh made her proposition to Gigo, "Will you help Toomas start a little business? We know you have had a great deal of experience."

Gigo looked as if her request had been a direct answer to a prayer. "But of course, Pertoosh. Nothing would give me greater pleasure," he replied with a glint in his eye.

The following morning Gigo took Toomas with him to the buisness district. First, he rented a small hole-in-the-wall space in an old building. Then he purchased a balance scale and a variety of dried fruits, including raisins, peaches, apricots, pears, and nuts. "Now, Toomas, the rest is up to you," he said. Toomas stood behind the display counter, appearing businesslike and most knowledgeable. Gigo stood to the side and observed. Soon Toomas was making many sales.

Shortly afterwards, wanting to show her gratitude to Gigo and Rozo for their friendliness and helpfulness, Pertoosh gave them four loaves of bread. She had splurged a few coins from her sewing and purchased some fine bulghur (cracked wheat) to make the bread. Although considered a "poor man's bread" it was, nevertheless, very delicious and wholesome. During these times of starvation they deemed themselves most fortunate to be able to purchase even a small supply of the flour. And they felt even more fortunate to have such wonderful friends as Gigo and Rozo.

The two were thrilled and grateful to receive the humble bread.

"Come to visit with us tonight," Gigo invited. Thinking how very hospitable Gigo and Rozo were, Pertoosh accepted.

But while she and her family were visiting them, Rozo sneaked away to the living quarters in the rear and stole all the bulghur bread Pertoosh had baked—twelve small round loaves.

When they went home, they discovered the theft. Utter amazement swept over Pertoosh. "Now who could have stolen our bread?" she asked. Victoria expressed shock. Toomas felt deep anger.

"I know who took our bread!" Toomas's words were full of fury. "It had to be Rozo, when she left the room."

"Who else knew we had the bread, Mama?" Victoria cried.

Pertoosh had to agree. It did not take a private detective to find out who the thief was. She came up with a plan. She invited Gigo and Rozo to their quarters for a return visit. While they visited, Pertoosh said she had to leave the room. She slipped into their bedroom and found all the twelve loaves of bread hidden under their bed.

She returned and said not a word. After the pair left, she said to Victoria and Toomas, "They took our bread, but we must not say a word."

"Why not, Mama?" Toomas wanted to run and beat up Gigo and his wife.

"If we try to recover our precious bread, that will only make them very angry and bring revenge upon us for discovering their theft," Pertoosh said. "Let them have the bread."

After the first wave of shock and anger had passed, Toomas agreed with his mother. Gigo was helping him in his "store" and they could not afford to jeopardize the business.

In spite of the theft, in the days that followed Toomas told himself he was the happiest "man" on earth. Every fiber of his being throbbed with satisfaction. Now he was truly the "man of the house," the breadwinner. He arose at dawn each morning, removed the key to the store from under his pillow, and slipped it into one of his many vest pockets. Oh yes, all the successful merchants wore vests with many pockets. He placed a long pencil in one pocket so that half of it would show. That was the mark of a real merchant!

He threw a shoe on the floor, making a loud thud—this for the benefit of his mother and sister who were still in bed. He had to let them know that the promising merchant was about to leave for his day of big business.

Breakfast? No time. He couldn't afford to miss a single customer. He placed a piece of dry bulghur bread in a pocket to munch on the way to the store.

How fortunate they were to have met Gigo!

His seemingly good fortune turned out to be short-lived, however, for in reaching to grasp a flimsy straw, they had embraced a viper. Toomas soon discovered the reason for Gigo's extreme willingness to set him up in business.

One morning Gigo instructed him to go on an errand several miles from the store. Toomas protested, "But Gigo, that is many miles. It will take me most of the day."

Gigo gave him a fierce look. "Do as I tell you," he ordered. "Go! Now!"

Many hours later Toomas returned. One glance at Gigo filled him with shock. There he stood, a hulk of a man, with disheveled hair and bleary eyes, wobbly on his feet. All around the room were many bottles which had held alcoholic beverages.

For a moment Toomas stood rooted to the spot, not believing what he saw. When Gigo saw him, he snarled, "Wh—wh—what are you staring at?" Toomas smelled the alcohol on his breath and turned away, tears stinging his eyes. The ugly scene made him think of his father, Garabed, and how much Garabed had hated alcohol and what it did to men, and Toomas knew at that moment that he hated it too.

Then he suddenly realized that all of his merchandise had vanished, and his shock quickly turned to anger. He shouted, "What have you done with my stock?"

Gigo gave a drunken laugh. "Sold it. That's what. Bought all these bottles," he boasted.

"How dare you?" Toomas cried, the tears streaming down his cheeks. "The stock belonged to me."

Gigo lunged toward him. Toomas turned and ran, crying all the way home. Wait till his mother heard about this.

Pertoosh grieved when she heard the story. She placed her arms around Toomas and held him close. "My poor child. How disappointed you must be. If only Papa were alive."

"How could he do it, Mama? We trusted him so." Toomas tasted his salty tears, which began afresh.

"Underneath his false veneer, he is a vile man. And he has a trigger-edge temper. We hear how he and his wife fight." Pertoosh caressed his curly hair.

Toomas had heard the fights. Hardly a day passed by without a fighting scene—pulling hair, slapping, kicking, biting each other, throwing any object within reach. And oh, the foul caustic words and oaths!

"And Mama, I'll *never* understand how those two escaped the khandjar!" Toomas cried. He lifted his head and looked into his mother's face. "What are we going to do?" he asked.

Pertoosh kissed his forehead and said, "Nothing. That man is dangerous. One of these days he will receive what he deserves."

Toomas wished that day could be right now. But Mama was right; someday he would be punished.

In the days that followed, Gigo and Rozo showed their belligerence by forbidding Pesa to pass through their living quarters to visit Victoria. However, another Armenian tenant agreed to let him pass through her living quarters. The few Armenians who had escaped the massacre had grouped together and lived near each other.

Pesa wanted to attend to Gigo personally, for robbing Toomas and being so hateful to all of them, but he advised Pertoosh to move away first, which she was glad to do. She felt sure that Gigo was capable of doing them bodily harm.

They found two rooms in a large house and began to move. Since they could not afford to hire a *hammal* (carrier), Pertoosh carried the heavy loads on her back and Toomas carried the lighter ones. Victoria stayed in the newly rented house to receive what few possessions they had. The moving turned out to be an all-day job. At last, all had been moved and Pertoosh went back to bring a sack of ashes from the fireplace, to be used for making laundry soap.

Victoria and Toomas waited for her return. Darkness was falling and still she did not come. "Something must have happened to her," Toomas said.

"She should have been here by now," Victoria cried in a worried tone.

"I should have gone with her." Toomas started toward the door. "I'll go find her." He began to run. When he had gone half way he heard a cry. He stopped in his tracks and listened. Then he resumed his running as fast as his legs could carry him. Soon he saw her in the fading twilight, hair tousled, eyes red and swimming in tears, swollen scratches all over her face, as though she had been clawed by a wild cat. She appeared on the verge of collapse.

"Mama! Mama!" Toomas wrapped his arms around her and drew her gently toward a large rock. "Sit here and tell me what happened."

Through unchecked tears and moans of pain, she related the story. "I had filled the sack with ashes, and—was—about to leave—when Gigo and Rozo—jumped on me."

Toomas gritted his teeth with rage. Pertoosh continued, "They knocked—the sack down—and beat me." Another moan escaped her lips.

"Did anyone see them?" Toomas asked.

"Yes, there were other tenants watching, but they were afraid to interfere," Pertoosh replied.

Poor Mama! She had been shuttling back and forth all day with heavy loads and had been too tired to defend herself.

Toomas took his mother home, helping her gently with every step. Once home, Victoria took over and Toomas left the house. He would show that Gigo and Rozo! They couldn't get away with this! His feet went in the direction of their house. Then something inside said, "Toomas, what can you do? You are small and both of them could easily overpower you."

If only Garabed could have been there—and Dada Toomas. Why, the both of them would have torn the two cowardly animals to pieces.

Toomas turned and ran in the direction of the hospital where Pesa worked. With tears he could not hold back, he related to Pesa what had happened to his mother. "Do not worry, Toomas. I will attend to them," Pesa promised, and at that moment, to Toomas he became both David and Samson, the invincible heroes of the Bible—and perhaps a bit of Garabed and Dada Toomas, too.

The opportunity came shortly afterward, when Pesa overtook Gigo on the street. He seized him by the collar and spat in his ugly face. He shook him as one would shake a tree for mulberries and was about to inflict a blow on the startled Gigo when a large hand on his shoulder stopped him. Pesa turned and faced the Armenian preacher. "No, no, you must not do this," said the man of God.

Out of respect for the preacher, Pesa gave Gigo a shove and released his hold. But before Gigo could run, Pesa warned, "If ever you lay a hand on *any* member of the Avedisian family again, *no one* will be able to save you." Gigo ran for his life.

When Toomas heard the story, he protested in disgust, "Why don't people mind their own business? Why do they have to interfere? No one interfered to help Mama when she was being beaten mercilessly."

Pesa consoled him, saying, "Don't worry, Toomas, I'll get him another time. There won't always be a preacher around."

Shortly after the incident, Pertoosh and Toomas went to market to buy cracked wheat to make bread. While Pertoosh inspected the wheat, Toomas looked around at the throngs of beggars, customers, and merchants milling around. All at once he spotted something that made his blood race. "Mama, Mama," he called. Pertoosh looked up. Toomas motioned for her to come at once. He had something to show her.

There at his feet were a man and a woman clad in the filthiest of rags, scratching the ground for a few grains of wheat. For several minutes mother and son stared at the wretched souls scratching and sifting the dirt. Could it be? These were the two who had robbed and beaten her, now reduced to begging. For a moment, a wave of sympathy swept over Pertoosh.

Yet it seemed that the words of the Bible were being fulfilled. Gigo and Rozo were receiving their just reward.

A happier part of the Avedisian family life was the romance between Victoria and Pesa. One day they announced their intention to marry. As far as Pertoosh knew, there was only one Armenian preacher in these parts who had escaped the massacre and who lived nearby—the same one who had stopped Pesa from striking Gigo. She went to him and asked, "Will you perform the marriage between my daughter and her fiance?"

The preacher gazed long and hard at Pertoosh. Then he asked incredulously, "Do you expect *me* to marry your daughter to that *Turkish* soldier?"

Pertoosh dared not tell him that Pesa was really an Armenian who had joined the Turkish army and posed as a Turkish soldier. That secret only she, Victoria, and Toomas knew and would keep to themselves.

"But he is a fine young man. Very kind. Not at all like the others," Pertoosh defended Pesa.

"No! No! Never!" the Armenian preacher's words exploded.

Later, Pertoosh had an idea. Why couldn't she do it herself?

She, above all, knew the sincerity of their intentions. By her words, she would bind them before God in a marriage indissoluble—till death parted them.

Late one night, while Toomas slept, she performed the wedding ceremony binding Victoria and Pesa in Holy Matrimony, with the Bible in her hands.

When Toomas woke up the next morning and found the couple already married, his disappointment knew no bounds. "Why didn't you tell me? I could have been a witness," he complained.

"God was our witness," Pertoosh said calmly.

Toomas felt the act of excluding him from the wedding ceremony was an unforgivable one, but now, happily, Pesa was his brother-in-law.

CHAPTER 28

Toomas Proposes Marriage

Three years had passed since the massacre. Events of the past seemed to be fading rapidly for the growing Toomas. Though only nine years of age, he felt he had experienced the life of a mature man. The time had come now to do one more thing that mature men did—get married. Fate seemed to be drawing him in the direction of matrimony.

They had moved once again, this time into a house owned by a kind, good-natured, elderly Armenian woman. To Toomas's great delight, the woman's granddaughter, Sacco, possessed all the charms of her grandmother. Almost at once, a magnetic attraction developed between Toomas and Sacco. They spent many hours together playing "husband and wife."

So natural did the role of "husband" seem to Toomas that he found himself wishing the relationship would become real. But first he must ask Sacco. While playing "house" one day, he blurted, "Wouldn't it be nice if we could really be husband and wife and have our own house?"

Sacco looked at him with big shining brown eyes and smiled. "Oh, yes, Toomas, I would like that very much."

"Well then, it's settled. I'll have to ask my mother first," Toomas said happily.

He rationalized to himself, why shouldn't they get married? Their fathers and mothers had been only a few years older when they married. What did a few years matter one way or another? Besides, marriage was proper and desirable. Hadn't Victoria just gotten married?

Besides, what excitement and fun the wedding would be! He recalled with longing the merriment at Victoria's first wedding in Hini, when Garabed was alive and Mama was happy. Oh, the good food! And the dancing! Waves of nostalgia swept over him. What joy for the children!

Back in Hini a wedding meant three full days of celebration. All the participants went to either the bride's or groom's house. Everyone dressed in colorful clothing and sang and danced in the streets. Every performer exhibited his best talent. Some had tambourines in their hands. Others blew sharply on animal horns. Still others made noises by striking anything they had with a stick.

But for the children the happiest time of the wedding was being hennaed. Custom decreed that brides and bridegrooms tint their hair with henna. The children were allowed to have their fingers hennaed between the knuckles and if they behaved, a dab would go on their foreheads. What fun!

As for the dancing, one had to be naturally endowed, a true artist, to be able to perform the Armenian dance. The dancer did not move to the tune of the music, but to the words of the song. He did not execute mere mechanized steps. Instead, he interpreted the ballad, the very song in the air, with quiet gestures and subtle movements of the body. He let the words of the song permeate his entire system. Then he articulated responsively with slow, agile, graceful movements, imparting a sense of tranquility.

Each word was symbolically expressed, as though his muscles from head to toes were in vibratory motion, spelling and chanting words of love, charm and seduction. His words depicted the greatest happiness that can come to man and woman—to love and to be loved. The rich, flowing Oriental minor tones, the lure of the ballads, served to allure and intrigue the beloved. The circle of spectators kept time with their hands.

The performer sometimes made castanets of his fingers, and sometimes waved a silk handkerchief in each hand to create enticement for his beloved. He continued his seductive performance until his lover or admirer fell captive to his allurement. Then he ceased to be the center of attraction. Such a performer was the embodiment of all that was charming and beautiful in the spirit of the Armenians.

As Toomas reminisced, his heart filled with sadness. How he wished Papa were alive for his wedding. Of course, it would not be the fabulous kind of wedding that took place in Hini—nothing would ever be the same again. But life had to go on. He must go in and talk to Mama. All at once butterflies flitted in his stomach.

Toomas entered the house where Pertoosh sat sewing. Victoria sat nearby, knitting. Toomas looked from one to the other. No—he shook his head. This would be the wrong time; they were completely occupied in their work. If he came right to the point, it might be like thrusting his head under an ax! He knew his mother. His proposal might shock her, and she did not take kindly to shock!

Pertoosh looked up when Toomas entered. He avoided her eye. She returned to her sewing. Perhaps he had better approach Victoria first. After all, hadn't she recently taken part in the sacrament of marriage? Twice married, she would understand.

He walked casually past his mother and went to Victoria. He bent and whispered in her ear, "Oolo." He would come right to the point, calling her by his favorite name. "Sacco and I want to get married."

Victoria dropped her knitting needles and twisted her head to look at him with disbelief.

"What?" she exploded.

"You heard me! I don't want to repeat it," Toomas whispered.

Victoria began to laugh. Why was she laughing? Marriage was not a laughing matter. Was she ridiculing him?

"What will you do if you get married?" she asked, still laughing.

What a question to ask! Had he asked her what she would do when she got married? He felt anger welling within him.

"What do you think? We'll just play together."

"Aren't you playing together now?"

Toomas's anger turned to exasperation. What was the use of trying to make her understand? Besides, it really wasn't her business. What he did, if he chose to marry, was his own private affair! Papa would have understood, he felt sure. He had wasted his time going to her. He would go directly to his mother. She understood all about love and marriage. Better yet, she understood *him*. And she would not ask such dumb, embarrassing questions. Sisters weren't very smart, anyway.

While he consoled himself, he felt his courage somehow slipping away. He wished he hadn't talked to Victoria. He looked at Pertoosh, her head bent over the sewing machine which Pesa had managed to buy for Victoria. She seemed terribly engrossed in the quilt she was making. Would she be shocked?

Perhaps he had better do something to help absorb the shock. He would offer to help her with the sewing machine. He came closer, practicing the words in his mind. While he struggled for the proper words, the proper approach, Victoria broke in, shattering all his strategy. "Mama, Toomas wants to ask you something." She still had that stupid smile!

Now she had done it. Too late. He would have to spill it out. Fearful now, he said the words timidly, "Mama—I—I—that is, Sacco and I want to get married." There, he had said it. But why didn't the earth open up and swallow him forever?

Pertoosh's eyes blazed and looked as if they would pop out of her head. He had never seen her in such a furious state. All at once, he knew his words were the worst he could ever have uttered. He could not have committed a greater sin. Could not the wind have blown the fatal words into infinity before he uttered them?

But why had she taken them so seriously? Instantly, before he could get away, she leaped to her feet and seized him by the arm in an iron grip he did not know she possessed. She dragged him into the next room, almost pulling his arm out of its socket.

"But, Mama, I didn't really—really—mean it the way you thought." *What* did she think? No use. In her condition she wasn't listening. No amount of reasoning could persuade Pertoosh from her intention. Toomas saw that. He knew she was about to administer corrective chastisement, as only she could do.

There in that room Toomas received the worst thrashing of his young life. Pertoosh, bent on teaching him once and for all that a nine-year-old should never dwell on or entertain the most delicate subject of matrimony, did not stop until he saw it her way.

"Promise me, you will *never again* think of such a thing."

Over and over, Toomas cried, with gushing tears and painful seat, "I won't, Mama. I won't. I promise. Stop, Mama!"

At last, convinced that he had learned his lesson, Pertoosh released him. And Toomas, sure that no marriage in the world was worth the price he had paid, assured himself that he would never bring up the subject again—not until he was an old man.

CHAPTER 29

Off to Istanbul

Victoria and Pesa had been married for two months when Pesa came rushing in one day, breathless with his news. "Victoria," he blurted, "I've been asked by my superior officer to go with him on a governmental mission to Istanbul."

Victoria, shaping a loaf of round bread, looked up from her task, a surprised look on her face. "Pesa, you really *want* to go?"

"Yes, Victoria."

"But, why? We've only been married two months." She turned away, a hurt expression in her eyes.

"Victoria, my home village of Medz-nor-cuegh is only a day's journey away. My parents were massacred, but our home is still there." Pesa placed an arm around her waist.

Pertoosh had been nearby helping with the bread baking. Hearing her son-in-law's words, she stopped her work to face him. An uneasy feeling came over her. These were not normal times. Many soldiers who married under the hectic stress of war had left their wives and had not returned. Her fear was intensified because she knew that no legal papers bound Pesa and Victoria as husband and wife. True, when she had performed the ceremony and had asked, "Will you, Pesa, take Victoria as your lawfully wedded wife—till death do you part?" he had placed his hand on the open Bible and said, "Yes."

Now would Pesa, whom she admired and loved, turn out to be like the soldiers who had abandoned their wives? The look on Victoria's face told her she was thinking the same thing.

Pesa seemed to sense their fears. "Do not worry, Victoria. I will send for you when the opportunity comes." As he held her close, Victoria seemed to accept his words. But she, Pertoosh, must extract a promise from Pesa.

"Pesa," she began, "I believe you are telling the truth. You will not abandon my daughter. Let us bind this pact on the Bible.''

"Of course." Pesa looked a little surprised.

Pertoosh took the Bible, opened it to Genesis 2:24 and read, "Therefore shall a man leave his father and his mother and shall *cleave* unto his wife." She held it while Pesa laid his hand on the words and said, "As God is my witness, I will always cleave to Victoria, my wife before God and man."

Looking at the young man's sober face and hearing his words, Pertoosh could not help but feel satisfied. Pesa had convinced her and her daughter of his faith and integrity.

"When you arrive in Istanbul, will you try to locate my Hovsep?" A wistful look came into her eyes. It had been three years since Hovsep had left for Istanbul to be trained by the Turkish government, and not a word had been heard from him. Pesa had never met Hovsep, but willingly agreed to look for him.

He had been gone only a few weeks when word came that he had been stricken with influenza, the "Spanish Flu" of 1918, which had already swept across the world, taking millions of lives.

Victoria, panic-stricken, cried to her mother, "But, Mama, Pesa must *not* die. I need him. How could I go on without him? I love him."

"Yes, we all need Pesa. He has been good to all of us," Pertoosh said in a soft voice.

"We would have starved without him," Toomas reminded them.

"Come, Victoria. There is one thing we can do for Pesa. We can pray for him. Our heavenly Father will hear our prayer."

They knelt, all three, beside a bench, each of them beseeching God to spare Pesa's life.

Pesa wavered between life and death for one month, then, as suddenly as it came, the flu left him and he wrote that he was well. Shortly afterwards, he wrote that he had been fortunate in locating Hovsep, but not without much effort. He had searched all over the great city of Istanbul for Hovsep, but had not found a sign of him. He did not believe he would ever find him—it was like looking for a needle in a haystack.

One day, while traveling to his home village, an ox-driven cart filled with young Turkish orphans passed him. He glanced at the boys casually, when something told him to inquire of them whether they knew a boy named Yousooff (Hovsep's Turkish name). No sooner had he mentioned the name than he noticed the *arabajee* (driver) jerk his head and saw the color leave his face. Since he had never met Hovsep, he did not, of course, recognize him. Nor could Hovsep know Pesa.

Hovsep was afraid to reveal his identity. He feared that Pesa, dressed in the uniform of a Turkish officer, might be an enemy. If he revealed himself, who knew what might happen? He could be robbed of his freedom, or punished for he knew not what.

Pesa then spoke directly to the driver, "Young man, get off that cart and come with me." With terror-stricken eyes, Hovsep obeyed and followed Pesa a short distance from the cart.

Pesa shot questions at the boy. "Do you have any living relatives?"

"Yes," came the reply in a low voice.

"What are their names?"

"My mother is named Pertoosh. My sister is Victoria. And I have a brother named Toomas." Hovsep's eyes filled with tears.

Pesa took a letter out of his pocket. "Can you identify this handwriting?"

Hovsep scrutinized the handwriting, then said in a rising tone, "Yes! That's my sister Victoria's writing!"

Pesa smiled. "I have good news for you. Your family is well. And I am Victoria's husband. We were married several months ago."

A look of incredulous, enormous relief spread over Hovsep's face. Nervously brushing his hair back from his forehead, he said, "I'm glad to meet you, sir. What do you want me to do?" His direct gaze searched Pesa's face.

"I promised your mother I would look for you. Where are you staying?"

"In a Turkish orphanage," Hovsep replied.

"Come with me," Pesa said.

"I can't come right now. I am driving the ox-cart with the boys. But I will run away tomorrow night and come to you." Pesa told him where he could locate him in his village of Medz-nor-cuegh and they parted.

After three days of waiting for Hovsep to come, Pesa went to the orphanage and found him there. "Why didn't you come as we agreed?" he asked.

"The orphanage is going to issue new clothes for all the boys and I wanted to get my share," Hovsep explained.

"Forget the new clothes. I will get some for you. Just grab your belongings and jump over the wall, and I will meet you outside the wall," Pesa directed.

Hovsep obeyed and now he was staying with Pesa in his home in Medz-nor-cuegh, Pesa said in the letter.

Pertoosh was overjoyed when she heard the news. She had feared her son would be lost to her forever, if he had been educated and trained in Germany. Once again, God had heard her prayers that ascended day and night on her son's behalf.

When Pesa wrote again that he had placed Hovsep in an Armenian orphanage in Yedi Koola, a settlement in the suburbs of Istanbul, she rejoiced even more, and thanked her heavenly Father. She would one day see her son again.

And now another turn of events occurred. The Turkish government ordered all Armenian refugees to be returned to their own cities and villages. This piece of news did not please Pertoosh, Victoria and Toomas. How could they go back to Hini—to the very ones who had massacred Garabed and so many of their loved ones? How could they return to the house that would haunt and torment them? Life could never be the same in Hini.

Toomas protested, "But we want to go to America, not Hini!"

"Yes, Toomas, that is what I am praying for. If only we could receive word from Aghegsanter. The war will soon be over. Perhaps God will open the way for us to go." Even as she spoke, the idea seemed only a remote dream.

"If only we could go to some large city and get closer to America," Victoria said wishfully. America—the very word was synonymous with "heaven."

Pesa wrote to them suggesting that they state they were emigrants from Istanbul, not Hini. Then they would be transferred to Istanbul to him.

"Why not?" cried Victoria. "A wife must go where her husband is. We have the right by marriage to claim Istanbul as our city."

"Indeed we do," Pertoosh agreed.

"But how can we declare we are emigrants from Istanbul?" Victoria asked Pesa in a letter. All letters were censored before delivery, but the censors happened to be Armenians. It didn't seem possible that any Armenian with true Armenian blood would betray the contents of their letters, so they felt free to write back and forth with Pesa, waiting for his instructions.

Pesa, having worked for the Turkish government, knew the procedure and instructed them how to apply for and secure their

teskeras (passports for travel in the Turkish interior). The teskeras would certify them as emigrants from Istanbul.

They secured their teskeras, but another problem presented
itself. As Istanbulians, they should be able to speak the language,
but they could not. Every village and city, usually isolated from
any other, had its own peculiar dialect. Some dialects required a
twist of the tongue. Other dialects, though Armenian, were
totally unknown to Pertoosh and her family. Their own dialect
betrayed the fact that they were natives of Hini, not Istanbul.

Fortunately, the Turks could not understand all the various
dialects spoken by the Armenians, or else they would have de-
tected the scheme. Still, the little family suffered a few anxious
moments. Would the Turks somehow discover that they were not
truly from Istanbul and make them go back to Hini? The very
thought filled Pertoosh, Victoria and Toomas with chills of
horror. They prayed they would not be discovered.

They were instructed by the unsuspecting Turks to proceed to a
city called Mardin. From there they would be transported by the
government on a train to Istanbul. Mardin, a city located between
Diyarbekir and Aleppo, had the nearest train depot.

Toomas looked forward with feverish anticipation to his first
view of a *shomandaffar* (train). Since he had never seen one or
even a picture of one, he imagined it to be a very large animal, the
great-great-grandfather of an elephant, perhaps, or a dragon.

"What is it like?" he asked Victoria. "Is it bigger than a
dinosaur?"

Victoria laughed. "Well, it goes faster than an arrow."

"Faster than I can throw a stone?" (And that was pretty fast!)
Toomas stretched his imagination. "I have heard that every time
you open and close your eyes you are in another city."

Victoria hugged him. "You will soon see for yourself."

After everything had been approved by the Turkish authorities,
they began the preparation for the long journey.

"We will have to take along food for the journey," Pertoosh
said.

"What shall we take with us?" Victoria asked.

"Toomas, you get us several five-gallon cans. We will take five
gallons of our own Armenian cheese, five gallons of butter and
five gallons of ka-woor-ma." Pertoosh knew the lamb would keep
and would be appreciated by her children.

Scraping together their meager funds, Pertoosh purchased a
hundred-pound sack of cracked wheat, and one of flour. With

Victoria's and Toomas's help, she baked round loaves of bread and filled a sack to take along. She also went about the house picking up heavy mattresses, quilts and a few small Oriental rugs, for she knew sleeping arrangements would be their own responsibility. It would be a long journey, and though their belongings and food made a heavy cargo, Pertoosh felt they had to be prepared. Who knew how long it would be before they reached Istanbul and the safety of Pesa's care?

Toomas could hardly contain his excitement. Soon, very soon, he would set eyes for the first time on that elusive monster, the shomandaffar.

They hired three horses, packed their belongings on them, and joined a caravan for Mardin—to them an unknown part of the world. The fear of marauders was ever-existent, but they traveled unmolested and arrived in Mardin, a shrine-like city set on a mountain peak, two days later.

Upon arriving in Mardin, Toomas asked excitedly, "Where's the shomandaffar?" He pictured himself riding on its tremendous back.

"Not yet. Not yet, Toomas," his mother said. "Look at all the people!" The caravan leader shouted, "Follow me." He led them to a large enclosed churchyard.

Hundreds of refugee families, in helter-skelter disarray, had already crowded there. The families of women, young girls and children (all without fathers) clustered about their own heaped up belongings. All of them had been waiting for hours, some for days and even weeks.

"What are they waiting for?" Pertoosh asked the caravan leader.

"They are waiting for their surnames to be called. When they are called, they will leave for the train," he explained.

"Where is the train?" Toomas asked eagerly.

"About a half day's journey from here, at the base of the mountain."

Toomas felt his heart leap. Only a half-day's journey. Then he would see it—the large monster. He could hardly wait.

A clerk took their names from their teskeras and told them to wait until they had been called. As time went by, it became apparent that they would have a long wait. After several hours, Toomas made a suggestion. "Mama, why do we have to wait?

Why don't we go to where the trains are and wait there?"

"Because we have been told to wait here," she replied wearily.

Victoria caught Toomas's spirit. "Mama, perhaps Toomas is right. If we have to wait, why do we not go and wait where the trains are?"

Pertoosh looked at Victoria, then at Toomas. She detested the waiting as much as they. Why not? She had always been a leader. Besides, being present at the train station would assure that they would not be left behind. Impulsively, she said, "Why not?"

Toomas threw his hat into the air with shouts of joy. He knew his mother was a leader, possessing some spirit which knew no fear, iron nerves that would not shatter, and indomitable fortitude. Everywhere she went, she commanded respect.

They needed to find donkeys to hire to carry them to the train. Toomas eagerly volunteered to find some, and Pertoosh agreed to let him go. A few hours later he returned with a guide and three donkeys. After packing the animals as fast as they could, they left for the base of the mountain. Several families saw what they had done and followed them.

The road wound through a tortuous mountain pass, very steep in places. The heavily laden donkeys advanced in single file, winding their way through the dangerous passage with a great deal of difficulty. The bulging packs on the animals scraped against huge boulders which jutted from the mountainside.

Toomas held his breath as he looked down at the awesome abyss thousands of feet beneath them. At times there was only an inch of dirt between the donkeys' hoofs and sheer oblivion below. The animals appeared sure-footed and Toomas was grateful that they had had many years of experience traversing the incredibly dangerous mountain paths.

When they began to descend, the guide pointed to the bare, desert-like valley, where a dark snake-like object stood.

"What is it?" Toomas shouted. "Could it be? Is it—?" The guide nodded his head. "Yes, that's the shomandaffar."

"The shomandaffar!" Toomas screeched. But why was it so very still, so motionless? It should be thrashing about, full of life. They had said it had the speed of lightning. He couldn't imagine a super-sized animal lying there inert, lifeless.

"Why doesn't it move?" he cried, his voice full of disappointment. "Why is it so dark? So strange?"

Finally, Pertoosh came to the rescue. "Toomas," she explained, "a shomandaffar is not an animal. It is a vehicle for carrying people and things."

Toomas felt his mouth drop open. "A vehicle? Like an automobile or a truck? It's not an animal?"

Pertoosh smiled and nodded.

Toomas shook his head with disbelief. He had come face to face once again with one of life's unbelievable mysteries. What a dupe he had been!

CHAPTER 30

Trouble in the Shomandaffar

When the donkeys came to a halt Toomas jumped down, leaving his mother and sister. "I'm going to see the shomandaffar," he called. Before they could reply, he was on his way, determined to unravel the mystery of this thing.

First to be marveled at was the length of it. There were eight sections (freight cars). What a long "vehicle"! He walked around and around the sections, examining every part. He counted the wheels and whistled. And what were the unbroken twin iron lengths that lay on the ground underneath? He climbed on the roof of the first car and jumped from car to car. He tried hanging from its sides. It might not be a living animal, but it was certainly a wood and steel monster! Never in his life had he felt so magnetized by anthing. It was even more astounding and mysterious than the automobile and the electric lights.

What made it move? The mystery deepened. Someone said that these sections were only the body. Its head was missing. If it had a head, it had to have a tail. The tail, too, was missing. While he probed and scrutinized, looking for answers, he heard his mother calling. He turned to see that she and Victoria had arrived at the train.

"Toomas, come help us carry our things," Pertoosh called, as she began a survey of the cars.

"What are we going to do?" Toomas asked.

"It looks as though no one is here. It would do no harm to move our things into the shomandaffar," she replied.

"It looks like we can have our choice of cars," Victoria added.

They chose one of the best corners in a car and spread out their belongings, giving themselves ample space so they would not be crowded. They could not know, of course, that such luxury was not for them, that they would ride the way of all migratory refugees—on the roof.

While they settled themselves into the car, they observed a caravan of refugees streaming toward the train. Some rode horseback, others were on overloaded mules. Many walked beside their packs, and several, suffering from physical exhaustion and bleeding feet, had wrapped themselves, like an octopus, around the back of some family member. Mothers carried their exhausted children, two or three at a time, bending under the load. A few walked freely.

The stream of shabby refugees began to fill the cars, until every inch and corner was covered. Pertoosh, Victoria and Toomas found themselves being pushed and crushed. Gone was their spacious domain.

"I feel like I'm suffocating," Victoria cried, elbowing her way for more room.

"Me, too," Toomas gasped, trying to catch a breath.

"How foolish of us to think we could have a large portion of the car," Pertoosh cried, fanning herself with a handkerchief. The day had been a hot one, and the heat from so many bodies was making the car unbearable. Still, Pertoosh told herself she was glad they were traveling in summer, instead of winter.

All at once, Toomas said in a whisper, "Mama, look at that man. Don't we know him?" He pointed to a man in the uniform of a Turkish general, who was pushing his way among the refugees.

Both Pertoosh and Victoria turned to look. Quickly they ducked their heads. "Yes," whispered Pertoosh. "That general came to Hini often and has been to our house many times."

"If I remember correctly," Victoria added, "he called us by our first names."

"Yes," Pertoosh pushed Toomas's head down. "We must not let him see us. He will know we are not residents of Istanbul."

"He will be sure to recognize us," Victoria said under her breath.

"Oh, why didn't we notice him before?" Pertoosh asked.

"We should have noticed his uniform and epaulette," Victoria whispered, covering her face with her veil.

"If we hadn't been so busy trying to keep our place we would have noticed him," Toomas cried.

"Too late now!" Victoria tried to sound calm.

Pertoosh wondered how they could possibly keep him from noticing them. It appeared he had stationed himself in their car. There would be no escape now. They would need to leave the car for water. Then he would surely see them. Only another miracle would save them now. She closed her eyes and prayed for that miracle. "No, Lord, *not* Hini," she prayed. "Send us to Istanbul."

"If only the train would move," Toomas interrupted her thoughts. "Then even if he recognizes us, we'll be on our way."

The train did not move that day, nor the next day. While they did all in their power to keep the general from noticing them, they discovered at length that their fears had been in vain. The general seemed not to notice them at all. He seemed quite preoccupied with his own thoughts, completely oblivious of their presence.

"He must have some important mission on his mind," observed Pertoosh, as she sliced cheese for their lunch the next noonday.

"Yes, he won't bother with us," Toomas said, tearing a piece of bread to eat with his cheese, completely unsuspecting that he himself would soon be instrumental in drawing the general's attention directly to them.

After lunch Pertoosh said, "Toomas, take the bucket and go get us some water." Toomas, happy to get out of the car, took the bucket and headed for the spring nearby. He had gone only a short distance when he noticed several small metal blocks on the ground. He bent down and picked one up. He had never seen anything like this before, he thought to himself, frowning. What was it?

Carefully, he examined it, turning it over and over. He saw that inside was a bolt attached with a short, sharp needle. He tested its sharpness by pricking his skin. It was sharp. The needle encircled a spiral spring. All the parts were screwed to the metal block which was about one inch in diameter. To Toomas, the metal block looked like an unperforated nut, much like a percussion cap. He stood there for a moment, completely baffled. Oh well, he would take one to Pertoosh. Maybe she would know what it was. He slipped the metal block in his pocket.

Upon returning with the bucket of water to the car, he looked for his mother. Of all things, she was in deep conversation with—he couldn't believe it—the Turkish general. And the general seemed quite friendly. Ah, we are safe, thought Toomas. He wanted to show her the metal block, but to interrupt would have been impertinent—a crime which brought dire punishment. He decided to show it to Victoria, but she didn't know what it was, either, so he placed it for safekeeping in the tin cup which was their drinking cup and hung it on the nail in their corner of the car. Then he went out to play.

Pertoosh, seeing that Toomas had brought the drinking water, asked Victoria to bring a drink for the general. Victoria took the tin cup from the nail and picked up the bucket of water. She smiled as she approached the general, and he looked pleased.

Victoria bent over to place the bucket on the floor, and as she did so the metal block which Toomas had deposited in the tin cup went hurtling to the floor, landing squarely on the head of one of the bolts which held the floor of the car. Instantly, the metal block exploded.

In the meantime, outside, Toomas had hardly gone thirty yards when he heard a deafening blast, like that of a powerful gunshot or a cannon blast. The explosion stopped him in his tracks. He turned and saw a cloud of dense blue smoke mushrooming under their car. What could it be? He felt his heart racing madly. A gun blast? In their car? A violent commotion had already started. Women screamed. Children cried. He ran in the direction of the car. Mama! Victoria! Were they all right?

He pushed his way through the mass of women and children. He must get to his mother and sister. When he reached them, he found Pertoosh on her knees before the enraged general, offering every kind of explanation she could think of. The general seemed not to hear a word. Eyes sparking with fire, mouth frothing, he shouted to Pertoosh, "You—Pertoosh Avedisian—have explosives hidden in your possessions."

Pertoosh shook her head. "No, no, general—there is some mistake and some explanation. You will see."

Turning to Victoria, who was shaking from the shock of the explosion and from fright, he snarled and spat the accusation, "And you—you had it on your person when you brought the water. You purposely dropped it at my feet."

Victoria burst into tears, "No, no, general. I knew nothing about it." The general's ears seemed to be made of stone. He would not listen.

Pertoosh tried to reason with him, "General, would we have done this to ourselves? We were on the same spot, too. Please listen to us." The general continued to froth and accuse. The impact of the explosion seemed to have transformed him into a ball of gnarled nerves. Pertoosh turned and saw Toomas. In that moment an electric spark passed between them. Instantly she was upon him, drawing him to the floor without ceremony, without explanation.

Toomas, already in a state of shock from what had happened, shouted, "What have I done?" From the look in his mother's eyes, he knew whatever he was being accused of was a heinous thing.

With heavy steel hands Pertoosh struck blow after blow on Toomas's buttocks, while he yelled, "Mama, I didn't do it. I didn't do it." The louder he yelled, the harder she struck, sometimes pinching his arms and legs with what seemed like iron fingers.

The angry general watched the severe punishment being administered to the culprit. Toomas knew his mother would not stop until the general's compassion had been aroused and he intervened to stop her. Had he no heart? Why was it taking so long?

After what seemed an eternity, the general, whose anger must have been appeased, placed a restraining hand on Pertoosh's shoulder. Then he went outside. Pertoosh released her hold on Toomas, who sobbed wildly at the injustice that had been inflicted upon him.

"Honestly, Mama, I didn't do anything." He pleaded with her to believe him.

"Then how did it happen? The thing dropped from the tin cup that Victoria brought to give the general a drink."

Between sobs, Toomas said, "That was a little metal thing that I found on the tracks. There are more out there. Do you want me to show the general? He touched his sore bottom gingerly. Would he ever be able to sit again?

A surprised look came into Pertoosh's eyes, as if to say, "Have I misjudged you?" That made Toomas feel a little better. He did not enjoy the role of the guilty party.

"Yes, Toomas, let's go find the general and you show him."

The general was walking around outside, a set and sober look on his face. Pertoosh called to him, "General, please, Toomas has something to show you."

Toomas led him to the spot where he had found the metal blocks. To his delight, they were still there where he had left them. He picked one up. "See, see, general. Here they are!" He handed it to the general, who took one look and said, "This is a *hand grenade!*"

Toomas explained how he had found it and, not knowing what it was, had deposited it in the cup, and how Victoria had not noticed it there. "I'm sorry, general, very, very sorry," he said, still sniffling.

The general looked at the tear-stained little face. Gone were his anger and false accusations, and he placed an arm around Toomas's shoulders. "I'm sorry it happened, too, Toomas. But perhaps it was for the best. Actually, I should be grateful to you. These explosives could have blown up the train when it passed over them."

Toomas smiled. Already he felt a little better. Pertoosh was looking at him and smiling, as though a reward awaited him. The general continued, "I'm sorry for the beating you took. That should not have happened, for you are our hero for the day."

Toomas couldn't believe his ears. From saboteur to hero—all in one day. Best of all, the general was no longer angry with them, and they could still go to Istanbul.

And the greatest wonder of all was that the explosion had not torn a limb or two from the general or anyone standing close. It had not even blown a hole in the floor of the car, or shattered the door. A miracle indeed.

Again, such a miracle must be a result of Mama's prayers.

CHAPTER 31

Forged Teskeras

Early on the morning of the fourth day, Toomas awakened to hear the cry, "The head of the shomandaffar has arrived." The sun's rays were already streaming through the open door of their car. Toomas reached for his shoes, buried under what seemed like tons of belongings. He must hurry to see the "head." They said it was the power in the head that made the train run.

Seeing Toomas's haste, Pertoosh asked, "Where are you going?" She was folding the little mat he had been sleeping on.

"To see the head of the shomandaffar," Toomas replied.

A broad grin covered Pertoosh's face. "Just be careful that it doesn't bite you," she cautioned.

Bite? Was it really a living thing? Without waiting to eat the piece of bread and butter that was his usual breakfast, he elbowed his way out of the car. Outside, so many people had crowded around the head that it was impossible for Toomas to see it. However, he had achieved a degree of expertise in squeezing his way through throngs of people, and he employed his push-through calisthentics until there he was, up front, staring at the head of the train.

He could not believe his eyes. While he had not expected to be "bitten," he had expected to see something spectacular, something that might even take his breath away. Instead, what met his eyes was a rudely constructed mass of wood and iron, shaped like the section of the shomandaffar they were occupying, with something they called an "engine."

Toomas felt pangs of disappointment. True, he was not a knowledgeable grownup, but even he could see that the thing needed countless replacements and repairs. How could it really have the power to pull all the sections to Istanbul? He shook his head. No way. Better go back and tell his mother about this.

When he arrived back at the car, he found Pertoosh and Victoria packing. Word had been given that all the refugees were

to vacate the cars. They would ride to their destination on the
roof.

Victoria cried, "How will we be able to hold on to our belongings on the roof?" She looked at the sacks and piles.

Toomas came up with an idea. "I know, we'll tie our belongings to the plank on the roof and hang on to it." Pertoosh thought
the idea was a good one, and they hurried to get themselves
settled. From the number of women and children who already
fought and clamored for a place on the roof of the shomandaffar,
it appeared that they were fortunate even to secure a spot.

With much effort and as much haste as possible, they tied their
belongings, and then sat down beside the loaded plank. When the
train started, they clung to their bedding and sacks and cans, lest
anything be blown or pushed away into space.

The train made many stops. Riding on the roof, under the
blazing sun, they sweltered, along with all the others. When the
train stopped, Toomas said to his mother, "I'll take our pail and
go get water at the public fountain."

Pertoosh wiped her steaming forehead with her veil. "Yes,
Toomas, but please hurry. We don't know how long the train will
be stopped."

"And we wouldn't want you to be left behind," Victoria added.

"I'll hurry," Toomas promised. Then seeing a group of Near
East Relief workers with large sacks, he called, "They're passing
out bread, one loaf for each person."

"We can't leave our belongings," Pertoosh said.

"Don't worry," said Toomas. "I'll get a loaf for each of us." He
followed the long line of refugees who swarmed with jugs and
pails to the water fountain and then to the bread lines. When his
turn came for the bread, he pleaded, "Please, my mother and sister
are on the roof of the shomandaffar. They could not come. Please,
let me take some bread to them."

The relief worker searched his face, decided he was telling the
truth, and gave him the bread. Toomas snatched it, grateful for
this offering of the Relief workers, for their own supply of bread
was almost gone.

Pertoosh said it was "manna from heaven," for although they
carried wheat and flour to be used when they arrived at their
destination, there was no way to make bread enroute. And the
butter—Pertoosh had shared it with their fellow travelers, when it
became obvious that it would melt long before they reached
Istanbul.

It was not always possible to leave the train to obtain water and bread, so the refugees suffered from great thirst and hunger. Since they were never informed as to the length of stopping times, most of them were afraid that should they get off, the train would leave them stranded in the middle of nowhere, to perish. Survival was always their first thought.

Toomas, ever willing to help his mother and sister, became more daring than the rest. "I'll get off," he would say, "and bring back water."

"But hurry! Don't stop to play. Don't linger for a moment," Pertoosh would say. "You could be left behind, God forbid!" An anxious look would come into her eyes. When Toomas went for water, he always kept a sharp eagle eye on the train, sure that if it started without him, he could outrun it and catch up. Fortunately, he never had to try.

As they rode under the hot sun day after day, he often longed to leave their sun-baked post, to walk in the grass, to romp, to jump, to lie under a shade tree. Sometimes he would exclaim, "Look, Mama, there's a running brook. The water is so nice and clear."

"Oh, for a cool glass of water," Victoria moaned.

"Oh, for a nice cool bath," Pertoosh added, fanning herself. "And how I would love to stretch my legs." They sat in tortuous cramped positions for many hours at a time.

Occasionally, the train pulled into a station and the conductor said, "All refugees get off and wait in the train station. You will change trains here for your destination." Sometimes that meant a wait of several days. Although it meant carrying their heavy loads off one train and onto another, they were happy to get off the roof and walk around. Wherever possible, they were herded into barracks, always old and dilapidated, to wait for the next train.

Every moment of every hour was spent in a careful vigil— watching and waiting for the train. Their greatest fear was being left behind, so they dared not stray away, even for a moment.

After a few weeks of travel, the train pulled into the city of Aleppo. Here they stayed in a deteriorated army outpost where some of the barracks had already crumbled, and the rest were tumbledown. While here, they met several Armenian men disguised as Arabs in flowing robes, traveling with the refugees. One young man took a liking to Toomas, who showed lively curiosity in everything around him.

The young man offered to take Toomas around and show him points of interest. First, he identified himself to Pertoosh as an

Armenian. Then he said, "We will be here at least a week so I would like your permission to take your son with me to see the sights of the city."

Pertoosh searched his face. It was obvious she was thinking, "Do I dare trust my son with this young man?" Seeing her concern, the young man said, "I assure you, your son will be safe with me." Then he reached under his flowing robe and pulled out his teskera. He smiled and handed it to her. "Will you hold this for me till we return?" A relieved look came over Pertoosh. She reached for the passport and gave her consent.

The young man called Toomas's attention to things that to Toomas were new and awe-inspiring. Some he had never seen or heard of during his young life.

The high point of his tour around the city came when the young man said, "Here is a restaurant. We will go inside and eat something."

Toomas's mouth flew open. "A restaurant? What is a restaurant?" He had never seen one before. The young man laughed and put an arm around his shoulders. "Come on, you'll see."

Inside, they sat at a table. This alone filled Toomas with wonder. The young man ordered something in Turkish, and a dish of something yellow and wonderfully beautiful to see and smell was placed before him. Toomas stared.

"Don't just look at it. Eat it!" the young man encouraged.

Toomas took his first bite. "Mmmm—what a delicious taste!" Manna from heaven couldn't be more delectable. He gobbled the smooth, velvety, whatever-it-was lemony concoction until it was all gone.

His friend looked pleased. Years later, Toomas discovered that in that restaurant in Aleppo he had had his first taste of lemon pie, and he would remember the sensation of that taste the rest of his life.

The disguised young Armenian stayed close to Toomas and when the train arrived, traveled with them for several days. He proved to be most helpful. Every time the train stopped he and Toomas jumped down and ran to the nearest fountain for water. How Toomas envied him because he could sit on the roof without hanging on to anything, while he and his mother and sister had to clutch their belongings as though their very lives depended on them.

While in Aleppo, Pertoosh befriended three young Armenian girls who were traveling by themselves. The girls, fatherless and without any males in their family, showed fear in traveling by themselves. They asked Pertoosh, "Would you let us travel with you as your daughters—just until we reach Istanbul?"

Pertoosh replied, kindly, "Of course. You will be my daughters and travel close to us."

After the train left Aleppo, it stopped at the city of Adana. The station, however, was a mile away from the city itself. The word went around that the train would be there for quite awhile, and that tomatoes were plentiful and cheap in the city.

"Mama, let me go and buy some tomatoes," Toomas pleaded. What a welcome change it would be from their staple of bread. "See, there are a lot of people going to buy them."

Seeing the large group walking to town to buy tomatoes, Pertoosh said, "You may go, Toomas, but be sure to come right back. . I don't know what you would do if the train left you behind."

"Don't worry, Mama. I won't miss the train." Pertoosh gave him a precious coin and Toomas followed the crowd. It was true, tomatoes were very cheap, and he bought a whole gunny sack full for his coin. Then he started back with the other refugees. On the way, buildings and vehicles caught his attention, and he found himself straying from the group. He wandered from street to street, full of curiosity and wonder, gazing at the new sights, serenely enjoying every moment.

All at once, he remembered. The train! How long had he been wandering without regard for time? Panic-stricken, he remembered his mother's words. He pictured the train pulling away with all the refugess except him—Toomas Avedisian. He visualized himself alone—never seeing his mother and sister again. He would die of hunger or be killed by the Turks. He began to cry.

He wandered in one direction, then another. All the streets looked alike. And the stupid tomatoes! They didn't help. The sack seemed to hold him down like an anchor, its size about the same as his own. To add to his misery, as he walked, the juice of the very ripe tomatoes ran down the leg of his pants and into his shoes. The tears that flooded his eyes made it difficult to see.

"Please, God, don't let the train leave without me. Help me to find the way," he prayed fervently. Mama always said to pray when in trouble.

He came to a stone wall and stopped to lean his tired aching body against it, releasing his burden of tomatoes for a moment. By now, the tomato juice had completely drenched him. Hearing a commotion, he looked up and saw a crowd of people all going in one direction. They were all in a terrible hurry, seemingly intent on reaching a destination.

A glimmer of hope flashed before him. Why not follow this group? They would lead him, at least, to a definite place. He followed them without asking any questions. They had gone a distance when it became evident where they were going. The train station! "Oh, thank you, God. But please don't let the train leave without us."

As they neared the train, the women and children jostled and pushed to be sure they would board. Toomas, still clinging to the dripping sack of tomatoes, elbowed and shouldered between folds of large skirts until he came face to face with the train—and there, only a step away, were Pertoosh and Victoria, ready to board.

"Mama!" Toomas shouted, dropping the sack at her feet.

Pertoosh turned and Toomas fell into her arms. She clasped him and whispered a prayer of gratitude. "Thank God, Toomas, you made it in time."

"And *just* in time. A few more moments, Toomas, and it would have been too late," Victoria had to remind him.

Before the exhausted Toomas fell asleep that night, he thought, "I hate tomatoes. They are always getting me into trouble." He remembered back in Hini, before the massacre, the time his mother and two aunts were preparing to make tomato sauce. They always got together and shared the work of preparing different kinds of food for the three families. They had poured about a dozen baskets of tomatoes into a large kettle and were boiling it over an open fire in their courtyard.

Toomas and his cousin Dickran waited on the roof, two stories high, each with a cat in his hands. When the boiling process was at its height, Pertoosh lifted the lid to stir the juice. As she reached over to pick up the ladle, the boys, holding the cats by their tails, with a marksman's accuracy and timing, slung them straight into the precious tomato sauce. The beating they received after a long chase made them wish not only that their aim weren't so good, but that they hadn't even been born!

It seemed that he had only been asleep a few minutes when Toomas heard a voice shouting, "Next stop, Istanbul!" A wave of excitement passed over the passengers. They had waited a long time to reach Istanbul. The trip had taken nearly a month.

At the station in Istanbul, Pertoosh knew their teskeras would be very closely examined. They had succeeded thus far in hiding their identities as natives of Hini. Would they succeed now?

Again she prayed that the God who had preserved and led them would continue to be with them at this crucial hour.

When they arrived in Istanbul, they stood in line with the refugees, teskeras in hand. One by one the people were dispatched. Now it was Pertoosh's turn. With a smile, and a prayer in her heart, she handed the document to the officer. She saw he was an Armenian. He probed into the teskera, and asked with a quizzical eye, "So you are a native of Istanbul? Where are you going and who is your nearest relative?"

The moment had arrived. Pertoosh knew that the Istanbulians spoke in a twang by twisting their mouths. She opened her mouth and attempted to sound like a true Istanbulain by affecting a twist of her lips. "We are going to the house of my daughter's husband." She turned and said, "See, here is my daughter and my son." As she spoke, she saw that her attempt had only made her look ridiculous. An Armenian inspector nearby broke into a laugh.

She heard her heart thumping loudly in her ears. She met his eyes. She must look composed, unflustered. He gave her a hard searching look. Would he, an Armenian, expose her?

The inspector said nothing, gave back her teskera, motioned her on, then smiled knowingly. Victoria and Toomas were processed the same way. Pertoosh let out a fast breath and thanked God silently.

Once again saved by a loyal Armenian, they followed the other refugees, and were herded like sheep into newly constructed barracks already filled to overflowing.

CHAPTER 32

Toomas Goes to an Orphanage

Pertoosh, Victoria and Toomas remained in the barracks in Istanbul for several days while attempts were made to contact Pesa. By now he had been discharged from the army and lived in what was left of his childhood home in Medz-nor-cuegh, a short distance from Istanbul. The house had been shelled during the war, and only a portion remained.

Pesa wrote that the only furnishings he possessed were the mattress pads and covers which lay on the bare floor. Nevertheless, for him it was home, and he intended to stay there. He told them they were to come to him at once.

With the end of their long journey in sight, they were all anxious to see Pesa. Toomas could not contain his excitement. "Do you think we will see Hovsep soon?" he asked.

Pertoosh's eyes misted. "I hope so. It has been three long years. I wonder how he looks." She turned away, took her veil and wiped her eyes. "It has been a *long* three years." A faraway look came into her eyes.

"Yes, Mama," said Victoria, "these three years have been full of hardships and struggle, but now we are looking forward to a new life." She spread a pad and a blanket on the floor, looked out at the setting sun, and turned to Pertoosh. "Here, Mama, lie down and try to sleep. You look terribly tired."

A new life! The very idea appealed to Toomas, whose youthful vim and vigor bubbled over. "Maybe we can go to America someday!" He gave his mother a look of encouragement. Mama did look tired and worn out. "And when we get there, I'll become a doctor and take care of you." That brought a smile from the weary Pertoosh.

A few days later they arrived in Medz-nor-cuegh where Pesa waited for them and greeted them happily. He told them he had been looking for work but jobs were hard to find. Pertoosh surveyed the situation. She recalled a well-to-do relative who lived in Istanbul. "Perhaps this aunt will have work for me. I will go to see her," she said hopefully.

Pesa expressed his regret that he could not care for all of them at this time and offered to take Pertoosh to Istanbul to see the aunt, who expressed her joy at seeing Pertoosh and her sympathy when she heard that Garabed had been massacred. She said Pertoosh could work for her as her housekeeper—an answer to Pertoosh's prayer.

Pesa kindly offered for Toomas to stay with him and Victoria. Pertoosh looked into his soft brown eyes and told herself how fortunate they were that God had sent them this wonderful young man in their time of great need.

"I am afraid he will become a burden to you," she said.

Pesa appeared unconcerned. "Don't worry, Mother," he said, "we will manage."

But Pertoosh's foreboding came to pass, for it was not long before it became apparent to Pesa that he could not earn even the most meager livelihood to keep himself, Victoria and Toomas alive.

When they went to visit Pertoosh, Pesa made a suggestion. "There is the Armenian orphanage where Hovsep is," he said. "I am sure we could get Toomas admitted there for a while."

Pertoosh pondered for a moment. The idea seemed to be a good one. There, at least, Toomas would always have food to eat and clothes to wear, and it would remove the burden from Pesa and Victoria.

"I have not seen Hovsep yet," she said, "but, perhaps if Toomas is admitted, I will be able to visit them both one day."

"Of course," said Pesa. "Victoria and I will take you."

That seemed to satisfy Pertoosh. "We will go back to the village first and wait till arrangements are made," said Pesa.

When the time came for Toomas to leave, Victoria said to him, "Toomas, you are almost eleven years old now. We are going to let you make the trip by yourself. You will go to Istanbul first to Mama, then she will see you off to the orphanage."

Toomas was elated at the prospect of a new adventure. "All right. I can't wait until I see Hovsep," he said excitedly. "What do I take with me?"

"Nothing except a bucket of olives and a bucket of English walnuts for Mama," Victoria told him. "Be very careful. Don't wander around and get lost." She smiled and hugged him. "We don't want to lose you now."

"I can take care of myself," Toomas replied confidently. After all, he had taken the trip once with Pesa and Victoria, when they went to Istanbul to see Pertoosh.

The trip would take nine hours. He would go by wagon for five hours, then by boat for four. Victoria gave him the metal buckets, which had no covers, then she and Pesa took him to the road where they placed him on the wagon. She kissed him and gave last-minute instructions, "Remember, go straight to Mama's house. Do not go with any strangers." She and Pesa stood waving and Toomas watched them until the wagon made a curve in the road and they were out of sight.

For a moment, Toomas felt tears well into his eyes. He had never traveled a long distance alone. He was leaving behind his beloved sister and brother-in-law. And he was going to an orphanage. What would it be like? Would he ever see his sister and Pesa again?

He brushed away the tears. He had been the "man of the house" for a long time. He was too big to cry.

After a long tiresome ride on wagon and boat, Toomas found himself on the boat landing in Istanbul. Now all he had to do was find his mother's house. Pesa had said, "When you arrive in Istanbul, take a streetcar from downtown to your mother's house."

It was late afternoon and thousands of pleasure-seekers were returning home and all seemed to want to board the streetcars at the same time. Every attempt he made to board the car with his two buckets met with failure. Each time he tried to climb into the car, men and women jostled and pushed and shoved until the streetcar had filled, and Toomas remained on the outside.

Two hours went by while he tried to catch a streetcar. The two buckets had become two iron yokes which weighed him down and kept him from boarding the streetcar. Without them, he thought, no one could have prevented him from squeezing his way through! No crowd had ever been able to hold him back before this. A feeling of utter exhaustion swept over him and he began to cry.

It started to rain and suddenly it was night. Toomas felt his eyelids drooping. He could not stay awake much longer. He would have to get some sleep. It had been a long, incredibly exhausting day, and now he faced the night alone and hungry.

Buckets in hand, he started to walk, looking around for a place to spend the night. He found a deserted entrance to a building, dropped the buckets beside him, and stretched out on the damp ground to spend the night. A cold wind came up, driving the rain all over him. He shivered and wished he were with his mother. How he longed to be under her loving care.

He found sleep impossible as he lay on the ground, cold and wet and fearful of the possibility of being attacked. A thought came to him. Now that night had fallen, perhaps fewer people would be wanting to board the streetcars. Something told him to get up and try again. He stood on his feet and picked up the buckets. Then he noticed a man standing across the street under a light. The man waved to him to come his way.

Toomas walked in his direction, glad for his friendliness, for he felt very much alone. The elderly bewhiskered man spoke to him, "Come with me, boy. I've seen you trying to catch the streetcar. I will help you." He picked up one of the buckets and carried it. "Where are you trying to go?"

Toomas informed him he was going to his mother, and gave her street address. As they approached an empty streetcar, the man explained kindly, "This car goes across the bridge, Bosphorus, to the European side. Then it turns right around and comes back to the Asian side to pick up vacationers. It will take you right to your mother's street." He placed Toomas on the car.

Toomas thanked him and, wanting to express his gratitude more tangibly, offered him the two buckets of olives and walnuts. "Here, please take them. I am so grateful to you."

"No, no, boy. It was my pleasure to be of help," he replied kindly, and as the streetcar filled up, the kind old man seemed to vanish into the night. Toomas looked back, stretching his neck, but no sign of him remained.

He sat comfortably seated in the car with the two buckets beside him. Who was the old man? Why had he helped him? So many people that day had pushed him away. As he pondered, he remembered something his mother had often said: "God sometimes sends angels to help us when we are in trouble." Could it be? Had God sent an angel to help him? Without help, he could not have been on this streetcar.

He offered a silent "thank you" to God.

Soon he discovered that the streetcar was full of people who had crowded past him. They laughed and made fun of him, pointing to his buckets. Toomas knew' they were thinking he was a mis-placed urchin. "I don't care," he told himself. "I'm safe in the car and on my way. Soon I'll see my mother."

The streetcar made many stops until only Toomas and the conductor remained. Toomas had given him the name of the street where he wanted to get off, but the conductor had forgotten. "Where do you want to go, boy?" he asked.

Once again, Toomas told him the name of the street. The driver had taken him on a round trip. At any other time, Toomas would have been filled with excitement at such an opportunity. But now, tired, hungry, and cold, he wanted only to reach his mother and go to sleep.

At last, the conductor stopped the car at his street. Such relief and gratitude came over Toomas that he held the buckets before him and said, "Here, please take these for your trouble." The driver laughed and shook his head, no. Toomas stepped off and he shut the door behind him.

A stony walkway led up to the house where Pertoosh lived. Almost spent with exhaustion, Toomas, still carrying the buckets, had to stop to rest several times. But now, his heart raced. In a moment he would see Mama, and this thought pushed him forward. As he reached the house, he saw her head through the second-story window. She turned and he saw her face, the most beautiful face in the world!

In a moment the two were reunited. It had seemed an eternity. "Mama, Mama," Toomas cried, "it took forever to get here. I thought I would never see you." He flung his arms around her. Pertoosh clasped him tight to her bosom and smothered him with kisses. "Oh, Toomas, I thought you would never get here. I was worried thinking of my boy by himself in this big city."

Toomas smiled. "I made it, didn't I?" Inside he felt proud. Then he told her of his experiences and about the elderly man who had helped him.

"My prayers, Toomas. It must have been my prayers."

Then she noticed the two buckets and her mouth flew open. "You carried these all the way from Pesa's house?"

Toomas nodded. "For you, Mama. Only for you. If you only knew the trouble they caused me," he said with exasperation.

"You should not have done it. But I will bake something nice for you with the walnuts," she promised with a beautiful smile. "And now you must get some sleep." She led him to a clean bedroom, where she had already spread a mattress on the floor for him. Toomas lay down and dreamed of walnuts and olives, of streetcars and orphanages.

The next day Pertoosh took him to an admitting office for the orphanage. After the papers were filled out, the clerk said, "We will take Toomas to the orphanage now." The moment for parting again had arrived. This time for—who knew how long?

Pertoosh took him aside. Her eyes filled with tears. "Oh, Toomas, if only I could keep you with me." She wiped her tears and mustered a smile. "But at the orphanage you will have plenty to eat. You will meet lots of nice boys."

For the moment Toomas didn't care about food or friends. "Mama, I just want to stay with you." He clasped her waist as though he would never let go. How could he leave his mother with the soft brown eyes and beautiful face—his mother who had loved him as only a mother can love—and who had chastised him as only she could do? He could not let her go.

"Toomas, read your Bible. Never forget the things your father and I have taught you. Pray always to God. He has spared your life for a purpose." She fondled his face. "You will be with Hovsep."

Toomas looked into her eyes, melting with love. "I am going to America some day, and I'll be a doctor. You will come, too."

"Yes, yes," Pertoosh smiled. "God willing, that will happen." Then she gently unclasped his arms, and in a moment was out of sight.

When Toomas arrived at the orphanage later that day, he was placed in an isolation ward, along with ten other new boys, where they were to remain for three days. During this time they were given a physical checkup, and since most of them were covered with lice, they were placed in hot water tanks and steam rooms for delousing.

After the third day, they were given new uniforms and shoes. To Toomas's rapturous delight, he was issued a pair of black high-top shoes with laces. All his young life he had dreamed of owning such shoes someday. In Diyarbekir, how he had envied the Effendi's sons who wore them daily and took them for granted. Mama had said, "Someday you will have a pair." Now that wonderful day had arrived.

He held them in his hands, hardly believing his eyes. He stroked the gleaming black leather. He had been told that it was his responsibility to keep them polished and clean, and he decided he must not wear them right away, for fear of getting them dirty. Besides, they would start wearing out. So he placed them very carefully under his pillow in the dormitory for safe-keeping. Then he went out into the main courtyard where several hundred resident boys were playing.

Now he could look for Hovsep. He could hardly wait to see his brother, after more than three long years. He tried to picture what he would look like, and wondered if he would recognize him.

He walked into the courtyard and milled around among the many boys who were playing, talking, reading books, or just walking around. He looked from face to face, hoping to find his brother. Not one face looked like Hovsep, or seemed at all familiar. Perhaps if he went upstairs to the main building's administration office he could look down and get a better view of the boys. He spent several hours in his fruitless search.

Some of the boys asked him to play, but he wasn't interested in anything right now besides finding Hovsep. With hundreds of boys in the orphanage, would he ever find his brother? Restless and discouraged, he turned to leave his post. Suddenly he noticed an older boy, about fifteen, standing behind him, his nose in a book. Toomas stared hard for a moment. The boy must have felt his searing gaze, for he lifted his head and their eyes met.

For a moment they stood locked in each other's stare. That face. Could it be? Oh, but it was! That face belonged to his brother! All at once, they leaped into each other's arms, laughing gleefully.

"Hovsep! How big you are! I almost didn't recognize you," Toomas cried for joy.

"And you, Toomas, you are bigger, too! How could I have recognized you? How long have you been here? Where are Mama and Victoria?" For a half hour they stood there asking each other questions and expressing their joy at being together again.

"Come on, Toomas. Let me show you my ward." With their arms wrapped around each other, Hovsep took his little brother to his dormitory and showed him his bed. At least one hundred single canvas cots lined the wall. They sat on Hovsep's bed and talked for what seemed hours.

At last, Hovsep said, "Let's go to the office and ask them to let you sleep in my ward." The clerk in charge of dormitories agreed to let the two brothers stay together, and issued a cot for Toomas.

For the first time in his life, Toomas told himself, he was actually enjoying Hovsep's company. He loved his brother, of course, but had always resented his superiority. Besides, Hovsep had given him quite a few beatings in attempts to break his strong will, but now he seemed different. Gone was his air of command.

While they talked, a call went through the air, "All boys form a line in the courtyard."

Toomas asked, "What is the line for?"

"Inspection. Quick, let's go." Hovsep led the way.

Toomas looked down at his tattered old sandal-type shoes. "Oh, I won't pass inspection with these. I'll go upstairs and get my new shoes."

"Too late. Here comes the inspector. Stand straight and tall," Hovsep ordered.

The provost walked in front of each boy, his eyes searching up and down. When he came to Toomas, he stood there as if magnetized, staring directly at Toomas's feet—at his old, torn and soiled sandals. All at once, without a word, he raised his hand and slapped Toomas's face so hard that he almost reeled around twice. It felt to Toomas as if his head would come off and fall to the ground.

The shock and the pain were quickly replaced by intense anger and outrage. Who did this ugly toad think he was? And how had such a disgusting person escaped the Turkish khandjar? He was a bad omen. Perhaps that was why the Turks had exempted his life, so that he wouldn't bring curses upon them! That had to be why he was still alive!

Outwardly, Toomas said nothing, but he decided that the new shoes definitely belonged on his feet, not under his bed pillow!

Frustrated Boy Scouts

The Yedi Koola orphanage was ideally situated on the outskirts of Istanbul, the largest city in Turkey, which was built on seven hills and is one of the most ancient of cities. It has sometimes been called the "city of mosques" because of its many Moslem temples.

Toomas had been at the orphanage only a week when the word flew from boy to boy that a well-known four-star general by the name of Mesrop was coming there.

"Who is he? And why is he coming here?" Toomas asked Hovsep.

"Now that the war is over, he is coming here to organize the first boy scouts of Armenia," Hovsep replied, repeating what he had heard.

"But who is he?" Toomas persisted.

"He fought Turkish and Kurdish guerrillas with General Antranik," answered Hovsep. "Everybody knows General Antranik."

"General Antranik?" Toomas echoed. "Of course; he's famous. I remember the songs Mama taught me about him." He had learned the patriotic lyrics by heart and sang them often. Who didn't know the great Armenian general? He was considered by many to be the George Washington of Armenia. Now General Mesrop, who had fought by his side, was coming here!

When the general arrived, Toomas observed that he looked like a "real general," with many visible scars to prove his valor in battle. Tall, handsome, with a strong, well-proportioned body, he wore a handlebar moustache with the ends twisted up. It seemed he never smiled—yet underneath the stony countenance Toomas soon discovered a kind, sympathetic and wise human being—a great man.

After his arrival, all the boys between the ages of twelve and fourteen were told to gather on the main floor. Hovsep was fourteen and was elated. But Toomas was not yet eleven. "How I wish I was twelve years old!" he cried.

"Sor—ry!" Hovsep gloated with a superior air.

About two hundred boys answered the call and lined up inside the main floor facing the general. Several hundred others, under-age and ineligible, stood outside, cramming their heads together to look through the windows. Toomas, as usual, had managed to slither his way through the crowd and occupied a spot directly in front of a window where he could see clearly everything that was going on. To his delight, the general was facing him, and Toomas could hear every word distinctly.

While the general spoke, he used two signal flags to communicate the letters of the Armenian alphabet, showing the position for each letter. Then he said, "Raise your hand if you are able to show all the positions." Several boys tried. Some went half way. Some were able to do three quarters of the alphabet. None could remember every single letter.

When Toomas saw this, he could hardly contain himself. From his vantage point, he had been able to see and memorize the positions of the flags for all of the alphabet. How he itched to be seen—to be called upon! He jumped up and down, holding his hand up, hoping the general would look his way and notice him.

At last, unable to control himself, he rapped on the window. Instantly, all eyes, inside the building and outside, were upon him. It took a great deal of raw nerve, but Toomas wasn't worried; he told himself he had a lot more in reserve.

The general pointed to a boy near the window and ordered, "Open the window." As soon as the window opened, Toomas exploded, *"Zoravar, yes gurnom!"* (General, I can do *all* the alphabet!)

Would the Zoravar refuse such a challenge when all the other boys had failed? He went to the window and with one sweep pulled Toomas through, as if he were weightless. From the corner of his eye, Toomas saw Hovsep glowering at him. Would Toomas do some crazy thing to embarrass him? Toomas could read his mind.

Full of delight, Toomas ignored Hovsep. This moment belonged to him. He snatched the two flags and without hesitation positioned correctly every letter of the alphabet, leaving the boys gaping and the general at a loss for words.

The general looked out over the large group of boys and asked, "Who can sing an Armenian patriotic song all the way through?"

Instantly, Toomas's hand shot up. Again from the corner of his eye he saw Hovsep's fists tighten and shake at him. Unabashed, he spoke boldly, *"Yes gurnom!"* (I can!)

"Then sing one whole song," the general ordered. His heart stirred, Toomas sang all six verses of the well-known Armenian song, *Tarts-yal-pyletts*. As he sang verse after verse he saw a look of approval and pride creep over the general's face. He also noted Hovsep's threatening look of disapproval, which seemed to say, "I'll get you for this later, you little show-off." But Toomas did not care. He was enjoying this sublime moment; it was his to cherish.

To his wild delight, the general spoke to him after all the other boys had left. "Toomas, you will report to my quarters every morning at eight o'clock."

Without asking any questions, Toomas countered happily, *"Eye owe, Zoravar!"* (Yes, General!)

Toomas could not wait until he told Hovsep, though he guessed his brother would not take kindly to the whole thing. To have his younger brother perform in such a superior manner was odious to him, Toomas felt sure.

In the days that followed Toomas reported as ordered to the general's quarters, where the general taught him intricate drills and gymnastics. He also taught Toomas, who was musically inclined, how to play the snare drum. "You will learn the snare drum, Toomas, so you can lead out in drills and parades," he explained.

Toomas felt that he would burst with pride and happiness. To think that a four-star general had chosen *him* above every other boy was an impossible, incredible thing. It was worth enduring Hovsep's icy stares and listening to his chiding, "That's right, general's pet. Make those shoes shine! Keep your hat on straight!"

Toomas only smiled. Nothing could touch him now. Each day brought new rewards and accomplishments. The boys chosen for the scouting program were issued white caps to distinguish them from the rest of the boys. And to Toomas fell the honor of being the only boy privileged to wear a bronze emblem on the front of his cap. The emblem bore the inscription of a sunrise behind Mt. Ararat. Over the rays of the sun were the words, *"Partsratseer-Partsratsoor."* (Rise-Raise) Those words meant, "You rise first, then raise others after you."

Frequently, General Mesrop took the boys on all-day maneuvers in the nearby hills. Here Toomas shone his brightest as he led out with his drum, while the marchers kept in step. If only his father Garabed had been alive to see him!

Before the maneuvers, arrangements were made with the cook to send a good supply of food to a designated place. Hours of marching in the fresh air always perked Toomas's appetite. He looked forward to every meal, although he knew exactly what it would be—beans, bread and tea. It was always the same. Still, not one boy was ever heard to complain. To Toomas, each meal was a delicious banquet.

Back at the mess hall, after maneuvers, the boys sat at long tables. Before eating, they stood behind their benches, holding each other's hands, and prayed audibly, *"Hire-mer"* (Our Father), the Lord's prayer. No one ate a morsel before prayer.

Before eating, each boy broke his bread into little pieces and placed it over the beans in his dish. Then, starting from one end of each table, one boy took an empty plate (always placed there) and put it over his dish of bread and beans. Holding the plate firmly with both hands, he turned the dish upside down, so that the juicy beans would soak the dry bread. Then he passed the extra plate to the boy next to him who did the same thing and passed it on, until all the boys had turned their dishes over. This practice took place at every meal.

The boys took turns at setting the table, and best of all, cutting the bread. Oh, how Toomas waited and longed for his turn! For then he could cut the delicious round loaves into four reasonably equal pieces and, as he placed a piece before each boy, could bribe his friends for a few extra beans in exchange for a larger piece of bread. It was his privilege, also, to cut for himself a larger piece of bread. This being the custom, the boy whose turn it was to wait upon the tables was very much envied.

As time passed, General Mesrop divided the entire group of scouts into smaller units, or companies, of ten. He selected a leader for each company. While choosing the leaders, he called Hovsep's name. "Hovsep, you will be the leader of company seven," he announced. A pleased look came over Hovsep's face. He turned and gave Toomas a gloating look. He was a *Dasnabed* (leader of ten).

After the general had selected all the leaders, he stood before the companies and made an announcement, "Tomorrow morning, all leaders will report to Toomas Avedisian for training."

Hovsep could not hide his astonishment and dismay. Once again Toomas had the superior position. Toomas, of course, had already received his training from the general. Now he would pass it on to the leaders. Toomas felt sorry for his brother. He knew how much he resented having a younger brother as his superior.

Included in the scouts' training was the performance of skillful gymnastics. Since the orphanage was in a beautiful country location, thousands of people came by boat and train on Sundays and holidays to have picnics and to watch the boys perform their drills and exercises.

One performance was of a pyramid formation. Four husky boys stood side by side. Three medium-sized boys stood on their shoulders. Two smaller boys stood on the shoulders of the three boys. Then came the grand moment for Toomas. He climbed and stood on the shoulders of the two boys, on top of all.

There he stood, chest out, chin up, eyes forward, giving the brotherly salute of the boy scouts, conscious of the many eyes that were upon him. Now came the grand finale. Without looking down at the general, who stood below him, he jumped, fully confident that the Zoravar would catch him in his strong arms, outstretched and waiting.

Oh, the thrill of seeing the look of pride in his beloved general's eyes! Of knowing that thousands had been amazed at their gymnastic feat, with himself as the star! He raised his eyes heavenward. "Papa, were you looking?" How proud Garabed would have been.

Truly, coming to the orphanage had been the best thing that had ever happened to him. Mama was right. The orphans were provided with food every day. They could always count on their beans and bread. Hovsep, too, considered himself fortunate. Both he and Toomas had become prominent leaders in the orphanage, and enjoyed their roles. Toomas told himself that *nothing* could induce him to leave!

Day after day passed, each filled with activity and honor. Almost a year had gone by and Toomas had already seen his eleventh birthday, when something happened to disrupt the tranquility of his and Hovsep's life.

Pertoosh came to visit one day, her face glowing with happiness and her voice full of excitement. Toomas just *knew* she had something of immense importance to tell them on this visit. What could it possibly be?

Then Pertoosh dropped her bombshell. "Hovsep, Toomas, I have something wonderful to tell you," she began.

"What, Mama? Quick, tell us," Toomas urged, hardly able to wait. "Are you going to get married?"

Mama laughed. "No, not that."

"Dada Khazzar sent you some money!" Hovsep offered.

"No, no, nothing like that." Her eyes shone with anticipation. "It's something we have been waiting for years to happen. Something we've prayed about every day since Papa died."

Toomas felt the strings of his heart pull downward. Was it what he thought? The words tumbled out of Pertoosh's mouth. "Boys, we're going to America!" She waited for their reaction, while she clapped her hands.

"America?" both boys said in unison, expressing not pleasure, but shock.

The smile left Pertoosh's face. "What is wrong? Aren't you happy for this answer to our prayers?" Now it was her turn to be shocked.

At last Toomas found his tongue. "Mama, at any other time, this news would have been the best, most welcome news we could possibly receive. But now—!" He turned his face. How could he tell her?

"Yes? Now?" Pertoosh persisted.

"Mama, just when we have important positions in this orphanage you want to take us away?" Hovsep argued.

Pertoosh looked as if she could not believe her ears. Toomas hastened to add, "I am the most fortunate, privileged boy in this orphanage. The general has great plans for me. Don't you see, Mama? We can't go to America. Not just now."

Toomas rationalized with himself about the importance of their staying. Hovsep was a leader of a company, and he was master of them all! How could they leave now—even for America—which anyway was thousands of miles away and only something vague.

Besides, he told himself, he had been waiting for weeks for his turn to wait on tables. Next week would be his turn. Then he could have a bigger piece of bread, and bribe the boys for more beans. (Sometimes, to obtain a larger piece of bread from his neighbor, he told the boys to turn around and look at something that wasn't there, while he exchanged his piece of bread for the larger piece. All the boys played this hunger trick.)

With his stomach taking priority over his reason, Toomas

clung stubbornly to his decision. No! He would not go to America. Hovsep joined him in refusing to leave the orphanage at this time.

"No, Mama, nothing you can say will make any difference," Toomas told his mother.

Ignoring his words, Pertoosh argued, "Toomas, remember how you always wanted to become a doctor some day? Here is your opportunity to become a doctor in America, like your Amo Avedis and Amo Hagop."

"No, Mama, no. Not now." Toomas could not be tempted.

Pertoosh turned to Hovsep, a desperate plea in her voice. "Hovsep, don't you want to see your brother Aghegsanter? And you, Toomas?"

Toomas had always worshipped the memory of his brother in America. But now even that left him untouched.

Seeing the boys could not be reached by any argument, Pertoosh assumed a firm pose and left them. She found her way to General Mesrop's office and shortly after, the general sent word for Toomas and Hovsep to come at once to his office.

The boy who brought the message said the general seemed disturbed and full of urgency. "Better get there in a hurry," he said.

What could the Zoravar possibly want of both of them? Toomas asked himself. He could only guess. But he knew he could count on the Zoravar. He would not let them go!

CHAPTER 34

America at Last!

Toomas and Hovsep stood before the general in his office. He nodded for them to be seated. Any second now, Toomas thought, the general would say, "No, Toomas, I don't feel you should leave here. I absolutely cannot spare you. No one else could do the job you do. And you, Hovsep, no one could be a better leader than you."

And that would settle it for Mama. Instead, General Mesrop began explaining about the boy scouts in America. "Did you know that their organizations are the largest and best organized in the whole world?" A friendly smile crept over his usually stony countenance. Toomas felt his eyes widen. Hovsep looked surprised.

"No, sir," Toomas replied. "No, sir," Hovsep echoed.

"The opportunities for advancing to higher positions are much greater than here," he added persuasively.

Toomas and Hovsep turned and looked at each other. Toomas's glance said, "What is he trying to say? No, we *can't* leave here now. Not when my turn at the table is coming up."

The general continued to extol the great merits of being a boy scout in America, the wonderful land of opportunity. "You will be able to live at home with your mother, and still be an important scout. You will go to school and be educated."

As he talked, Toomas began to see a vision of America—the land of everyone's dream. He saw himself as a student, as a scout leader, and one day, as a doctor. From the look on Hovsep's face, he was seeing the same vision.

At last, the general saw that they had been convinced. "I am sorry to see you leave, Toomas and Hovsep. But the opportunities are so great for you that I will not stand in your way."

Toomas suddenly felt tears brimming in his eyes. Impulsively, he ran to the general, who had been so very kind and good to him, and placed his arms around his tall hero, laying his head on his chest. General Mesrop raised a hand and patted Toomas's head. "Will you write to me and let me know how you are getting along? I will expect great things of you."

"Oh, yes, sir," Toomas sniffed and quickly brushed his tears away. He did not want to appear unmanly before his general.

They said "goodbye" and shortly afterwards, with their mother, the boys left the orphanage they had grown to love. It had taken a four-star general to convince them!

Pertoosh talked happily about the events that had taken place in recent days. "Boys, we should thank God day and night that the war is over. My letter to your brother reached him, and after all these years, I have had communication with him," she said, full of gratitude.

"What did he say, Mama?" Toomas asked.

"Aghegsanter says he will send us the money to go to America!" Pertoosh turned to the boys and Toomas saw that her eyes were misty with tears—tears of happiness and gratitude.

"When are we leaving?" Hovsep wanted to know.

A shadow came over Pertoosh's countenance. "Pesa has been helping me by looking into the matter of getting our visas."

"Are he and Victoria going, too?" Toomas asked.

"Of course," Pertoosh answered, and looked pleased at the thought of having all her children with her. "But there is a problem. We can make the immigration quota, but the Turkish government will not allow us to leave from Turkey."

"What shall we do, Mama?" Toomas's voice rose with excitement. Now that they had left the orphanage, they *must* go to America.

"We will see. There must be a way. God will lead us, as He has done thus far," Pertoosh replied with an air of confidence.

In the days that followed, she went with Pesa and Victoria from one government building to another, from consulate to consulate, to see if there were one country that would let them leave for America from Turkey. Bulgaria, Romania, Greece—all turned them down.

As the days passed, it began to look as if all doors to America had been slammed shut before them. But Pertoosh would not express any discouragement. "No, we must not give up. We must keep trying. God has not brought us this far to abandon us now," she said.

More days and weeks passed. The first flurries of snow fell. Aghegsanter had sent money for their passage and living expenses. Toomas and Hovsep were getting restless and talked of going back to the orphanage. "No, no," Pertoosh said firmly. "Our God will find a way for us to get to America."

On a cold, blustery day, Toomas went with Pertoosh and Victoria to a government building to try again. While his mother and sister were inside, Toomas, who was always intrigued by windows, stood on the outside looking in. He never tired of seeing what he could see.

As he watched the clerks sitting at their desks and walking around the office, he noticed in particular a well-dressed, extremely handsome young man working at his desk. Somehow, he captivated Toomas's attention and admiration. The young man rose and walked around the office. Toomas could not keep his eyes off him.

Suddenly, as if pierced by Toomas's unmoving gaze, he looked up and noticed him. For a moment they stared at each other. Instantly, Toomas knew he had seen him before. Then, in a flash, he recognized him. It was his cousin Benyamen!

For a moment his mind slipped back to Hini. He had been very young when Benyamen and his brother Hovaness had come to Hini for a brief visit. Hovaness had graduated from a German seminar in *Mamuret el Aziz*, Kharput, Turkey. Later, before the war started, he came to Hini once again to teach in the Prostestant school. As a result, when the massacre started, Hovaness was among the first to forfeit his life.

Benyamen, on the other hand, had been in Mamuret el Aziz when the war started, to finish his education, and had thus escaped the massacre. Toomas had never forgotten Benyamen because he was the only one he had ever seen who could juggle three raw eggs, to Toomas a magical accomplishment.

Instantly, he was off to find his mother and sister. Though he couldn't believe it, it *was* true—that *was* his cousin Benyamen. When he found them, he cried, "Mama, Victoria, follow me. Come and see. Cousin Benyamen works here." He pointed to the window.

A look of disbelief came over Pertoosh. "Here? In this building?" Toomas nooded. "What are you saying, Toomas?"

"Toomas, how could you know cousin Benyamen? You were hardly more than a baby when he came to Hini," Victoria scolded.

"That's him. That's him. I know that's him. Look!" Toomas pointed his finger directly at the young man, while Pertoosh and

Victoria stood before the window staring. Benyamen turned and saw the three from the window, and in an instant he jumped from his chair, ran outside, and with one sweeping motion embraced all three.

"Aunt Pertoosh, Victoria, Toomas—what are you doing here?" Between tears of happiness that drenched all four, they asked each other questions.

"Oh, Benyamen, we are so happy to see you." Pertoosh kissed him over and over. "Aghegsanter has sent for us to go to America. But we have been unable to get a country to allow us to pass through."

Benyamen's handsome young face broke into a smile. "You have come to the right place. I'm sure I can help you."

"You can?" Pertoosh asked incredulously. "God has sent us to you. Bless you, bless you." She held his face between her hands, saying gently, "My dear sister's son, I can't believe it. I did not think I would ever see you again. And to think Toomas recognized you."

"It's another miracle, Mama." Victoria turned to Toomas and looked at him with new admiration. "If it hadn't been for Toomas—"

Toomas, of course, felt his ego inflated. *He* had been the one to spot and recognize Benyamen, and now he would help them get their visas for America.

True to his word, Benyamen, through his governmental connections, obtained visas for them to go to France. From there they would sail for America.

On February 25, 1920, Pertoosh, Hovsep, Toomas, Pesa and Victoria boarded a ship for France. Benyamen went to say "Bon Voyage." Pertoosh showered him with good wishes and blessings. They watched his manly figure from the deck, until he disappeared into the sky.

As the ship passed through the strait of Dardanelles, Toomas and Hovsep heard two passengers talking. One was saying, "They say the strait is full of mines. Many ships have sunk here. The war is over, but the mines are still here."

"Mines?" Toomas asked Hovsep.

"Yes, they are underwater bombs that explode and sink the ships. The enemy put them here during the war," Hovsep explained, appearing very knowledgeable.

"Will our ship explode? Are we all going to die?" Toomas couldn't believe that after all they had been through, they would die now. They were on their way to America, where everyone was free, and gold lay everywhere, just for the taking. A new world lay just across the waters.

The ship had slowed down to only a few knots per hour. Passengers everywhere had heard the terrifying possibility. They lined up against the rail and watched the treacherous water with fear-filled eyes.

Toomas ran to find his mother, who stood on the deck with Pesa and Victoria. "Mama, did you hear about the mines?" Toomas's voice was filled with fear.

"Yes, Toomas. But God has not led us this far only to destroy us now." People everywhere were praying. Pertoosh dropped on her knees. "Our God, you are a God of miracles," she said in a strong, calm voice. "You have spared us during the massacre. One more miracle, please, for all of us on this ship." She rose from her knees and faced her family tranquilly. "God is with us. We will get through safely." The sun's rays shone through her chestnut hair, giving her a radiance as bright as her faith. How like his mother to pray for everything, Toomas thought. Always, when she prayed, he felt the same peace that filled her.

The ship passed through the forty-mile strait safely into the Mediterranean Sea. Despite the winter storms, the sea looked placid and beautiful, and the rest of the voyage was pleasant.

In France they learned they would have to wait three months before securing passage for America. They spent one month in Marseilles and two months in Paris, in hotel rooms.

Toomas found life in a hotel room a boring existence. Filled with insatiable curiosity, he wandered daily to explore. His favorite pastime was window-watching. How he loved to see what he could see! Besides, hadn't window-watching yielded good things for him—Benyamen, for instance?

Mama always warned, "Toomas, be careful. Do not get lost."

"Do not worry, Mama." Hadn't he found his way around Diyarbekir, Adana and Istanbul? To insure that he would not be lost, he was careful to note easily distinguishable features on various buildings, such as a church steeple or drinking fountain, to help him find his way back.

One delightful spring morning he wandered around the city listening to the melody of the birds, noticing the bright flowers and enjoying sights he had never seen before. Magic seemed to fill the air.

As he walked, he marked the sidewalks on the corners with a

piece of white chalk, congratulating himself on his ingenuity. On his return, all he had to do was follow the marks, and voila! he would be home.

Hours passed, while he gazed in windows, observing many strange things. (Toomas did not know he could go *inside* the stores.) It was late afternoon when he decided it was time to retrace his steps by following the white marks he had made. To his amazement, no matter where he turned, they had disappeared. For a moment, panic struck him. Although he had learned some French, he was unable to converse with anyone to ask for directions. He realized now he was hopelessly lost. The more he walked, the stranger the sights. He was lost in the middle of Paris!

But he didn't stop looking into windows. He found himself in a downtown area, facing some flimsy curtains in a window. The curtains were so thin, he could see shadows behind them. Forgetting that he was lost, he stood before the window, captivated by the shadows. They appeared to be women, and to his shock, they were nude women!

He stood there gaping, not understanding. Didn't the women know they could be seen clearly behind those flimsy curtains? While he stared, a young lady, nearly nude, came to the door. "Go away. You are too young to be here." She laughed. Toomas noticed her golden hair—like wheat—and her painted, artificial-looking face and pretty eyes.

When he did not reply, because he was tongue-tied, she repeated, "I said, you are too young to be here. Now go away." Getting no response, she said, "You must be lost. Now go, before a policeman finds you." Though she spoke in French, Toomas understood her words.

If a policeman found him here, he thought, he might be dragged to jail for he knew not what, and he turned and began to run, hurrying past many windows with flimsy curtains and shadowy ladies. He ran right into the arms of a tall policeman. Before the policeman could ask questions, Toomas made him understand that he was lost. The surprised officer asked him where he lived and told him how to find his way back to the hotel.

At home he related his experience to his mother, Victoria and Pesa. Pesa whispered to Victoria, "Brothels." To Toomas he said, "Stay away from that area. Do you understand?" Toomas did not understand until years later. He had gone sightseeing in Paris's infamous red light district!

Toomas, who was always listening and asking questions,

found the French language easy to learn, but Pesa, on the other hand, found it difficult. He was getting a haircut in a barber shop one morning when the barber asked him in French if he wanted a shave. "Oui, oui," Pesa replied, this being the extent of his French vocabulary.

"Do you want a shampoo?"

"Oui, oui," Pesa said.

"Hot-oil treatment?"

"Oui, oui," repeated Pesa.

Whatever he asked, Pesa said, "Oui, oui." After the barber had finished, he presented him with a bill which Pesa could not pay. The barber called a policeman who settled it by saying to the barber, "You have taken advantage of this man," and Pesa did not have to pay the excess charges.

Weeks passed and Toomas continued to explore and indulge in his window-gazing adventures. He was fascinated when he saw people eating something he had never tasted—chocolate bars. They were sold in bulk, large chunks over a foot long. People everywhere ate them while they walked. One day, he took a precious coin that his mother had given him and purchased a chunk. The smooth buttery mellow flavor of chocolate melting on his tongue gave him an entirely new taste sensation. This had to be the most delectable taste in the world! He took some home to his family, who had to agree with him.

Long loaves of unwrapped French bread were sold everywhere. Toomas enjoyed watching the stacks of bread and inhaling their fragrance. He compared them with the round dark loaves of bread he had subsisted on for so long in Turkey, and found the taste of the white loaves refined and delicious.

As the time drew near for their departure, they were told to report to a health station to have their eyes examined for trachoma, an inflammatory disease of the eyes, which was considered contagious. Passports would not be issued without this examination.

Pertoosh, Hovsep, Toomas and Pesa were declared free of the disease, but Victoria was told, "You have trachoma. You must remain here three months for treatment. When you are cured, we will issue your passport."

Poor Victoria burst into tears. "How can this be?" she protested. "I've waited so long to go to America."

"Do not worry, Victoria," Pesa said gently. "I will not leave you. I will stay until you are cured." His words gave her comfort,

but she was greatly disappointed not to be able to leave with her mother and brothers.

On May 29, 1920, Pertoosh, Hovsep and Toomas boarded the French liner *Rochambeau* at the port LeHavre, France. What a day for elation and happiness! At last their dream was coming true. They were going to America, land of freedom and promise.

Victoria sobbed when she said "goodbye" to her family. Toomas tried to comfort her. "Don't worry, Victoria, I will become a doctor in America some day and will take care of you." She kissed and hugged her little brother and could hardly let him go.

While they waited to walk up the gangplank, Pertoosh expressed her burning wish, "I want to touch the ground, kiss it, and then die."

The voyage across the Atlantic Ocean, unlike the one on the calm Mediterranean Sea, turned out to be a tempestuous nightmare for many of the passengers. The mountainous waves rocked the triple-stacked ship to and fro, and it tossed about the ocean like a tiny canoe.

Pertoosh and Hovsep became uncontrollably seasick and spent most of their time on their bunks in the ship's hold. But to Toomas the rocking of the ship gave, not seasickness, but great thrills. "I'm sorry, Mama and Hovsep," he would say, then leave to ride the bow of the ship. He enjoyed every moment of the fourteen-day voyage. Never had he experienced such excitement and sheer pleasure.

At last the sea became calmer and one day the ship drew into the New York Harbor. Toomas could not contain his excitement. He felt his heart racing and his feet itching. He couldn't believe it. Heaven! They had arrived in Paradise! "Mama," he cried, jumping up and down, "there it is! There it is!" He pointed to the Statue of Liberty, standing high and majestic, on a small island. The upreaching arm seemed to beckon them with the words of the Jewish poet, Emma Lazarus:

> *"Give me your tired, your poor,*
> *Your huddled masses yearning to be free,*
> *The wretched refuse of your teaming shore,*
> *Send these, the homeless, tempest-tossed,*
> *To me."*

Pertoosh was already crying tears of sheer joy and gratitude. "Thank you, Father, Oh, thank you," she whispered. "We see the promised land."

Hovsep, like Toomas, could not suppress his excitement.

"Look at the tall buildings—so many of them, all huddled together," he cried, pointing to the New York skyline.

The ship docked and the passengers were taken by ferry to Ellis Island for inspection and baggage examination. The immigrants were processed in a brick and stone palace-like building, in alphabetical order according to nationality.

Each had to undergo a thorough medical examination. While Pertoosh and the boys waited, they saw that hundreds did not pass the examination and were told they would have to return to their old country. Some cried with agonizing sobs. To reach the promised land and not be able to cross over was a cruel, heart-rending thing.

"Mama, do you think we will pass the examination?" Toomas asked, fear choking his voice. "I don't want to go back to Turkey!"

"Do not think of such a thing," Pertoosh replied firmly. "it is God who is leading us."

"Think about Amo Avedis and Amo Hagop who are waiting for us," said Hovsep, trying to sound cheerful.

Many hours passed and it became apparent that since there were thousands ahead of them, they would be detained on Ellis Island for several days. Toomas found the waiting painful and wished there were windows around for gazing, but Mama said he must *not* wander around while they were here.

On the fourth day their turn came. They were stripped of their clothing and examined. All three passed the examination. Again Pertoosh thanked God, and Toomas told himself he was the happiest little Armenian boy in the whole world. America! A dream come true. What wonderful, exhilarating experiences lay before him?

At last they were ferried to the New York dock where the two uncles, Garabed's brothers, waited. Pertoosh and the boys fell into their open arms and were smothered with kisses and tears.

"My, what fine young boys," said Amo Avedis proudly. "Toomas, you resemble your father."

"Come, let us go home," said Amo Hagop. "You must be terribly tired and weary." He gave them a fond look. "My car is waiting."

Toomas felt a great sense of pride when he looked at his two uncles, both of them medical doctors. Some day *he* would be a doctor, too.

Amo Hagop drove them to his home in Boston. They talked

about Hini and the massacre. Pertoosh related in detail how God had performed a miracle to spare their lives and how He, in His mercy, sustained them after the war, and led them safely through hardships and trials, to the blessed land of America, where her wish had come true—to kiss the ground.

Toomas and Hovsep enjoyed every moment of their stay in Boston. Their uncles took them sightseeing and explained the history of the city. Wide-eyed and awed, Toomas still couldn't believe they were in the land of their dreams—the land of many opportunities. Scouts, schools, medical school—all to be savored.

They stayed with the uncles for three months. Then Pertoosh became anxious to see her son, Aghegsanter, who lived on a twenty-acre ranch in Fresno, California, and who was waiting for them to come there.

As the time approached when they would leave for California, Amo Avedis said to Pertoosh, "Toomas is a bright boy. He will learn fast. Let us keep him here. We will send him to school and in time he will become a doctor."

Pertoosh would not hear of it. "No, Avedis. I appreciate what you want to do, but I want to raise Toomas myself. My boys are all I have left now." Tears clouded her eyes. "God has spared us. There is a place, a work for us to do here in this blessed land. We will find it."

Toomas was happy for her decision. He and Hovsep would work hard to take care of her, to make up for the suffering she had endured, and some day she would be proud of them.

God had set them free!

Back in Hini, Dada Khazzar and Sopig Mama lived out their days, both of them living to their nineties.

Amo Krikor, the uncle who offered his life's services to the Madoor in exchange for the lives of his family during the massacre, stayed in Hini and paid his debt. Years later, after his wife died, he went to Paris, France and lived there with his two sons and daughter. He died in his nineties.

The aunt and cousins who went to Diyarbekir after the massacre wandered from village to village looking for work and managed to escape death by starvation. A few of the cousins found their way to America in later years.

Victoria and Pesa came to America a year after Pertoosh and the boys. Their marriage lasted forty years—until death came to dissolve it. They had three daughters.

Hovsep went to night school in Fresno, California, and worked on his brother Aghegsanter's farm there. Later he was married and worked in the family grocery store in Burbank, California for many years.

Pertoosh, ever grateful for and never forgetting what God had done for them, lived with her sons, working on the farm and later in the family grocery store. She loved every inch of her portion of the blessed land, enjoying its blessings for thirty years. She never remarried, and died at the age of eighty-five.

And Toomas went to school, advancing rapidly by skipping grade after grade. He also helped in the family store, later working his way through college as a movie stars' barber in Hollywood. His dream of becoming a doctor came true. He practiced preventive medicines, later specializing in endocrinology. He married and has two daughters, Barbara and Laura, and currently lives in Fresno with his wife Helen. At the age of seventy-one, as a result of a lifetime of clean, healthful living, he is enjoying excellent health.

Toomas's life has never ceased to be eventful. He has achieved the distinction of being the only person who can do the Single Leg Push-ups (an exercise of his own devising) more than three hundred times without stopping. He has demonstrated this physical feat in high schools, colleges, gyms and Y.M.C.A.'s all over this country, Europe and Asia, and has never been challenged by anyone who could do it even once with each leg. Hence, he claims to be the world champion of Single Leg Push-ups. That's Toomas!

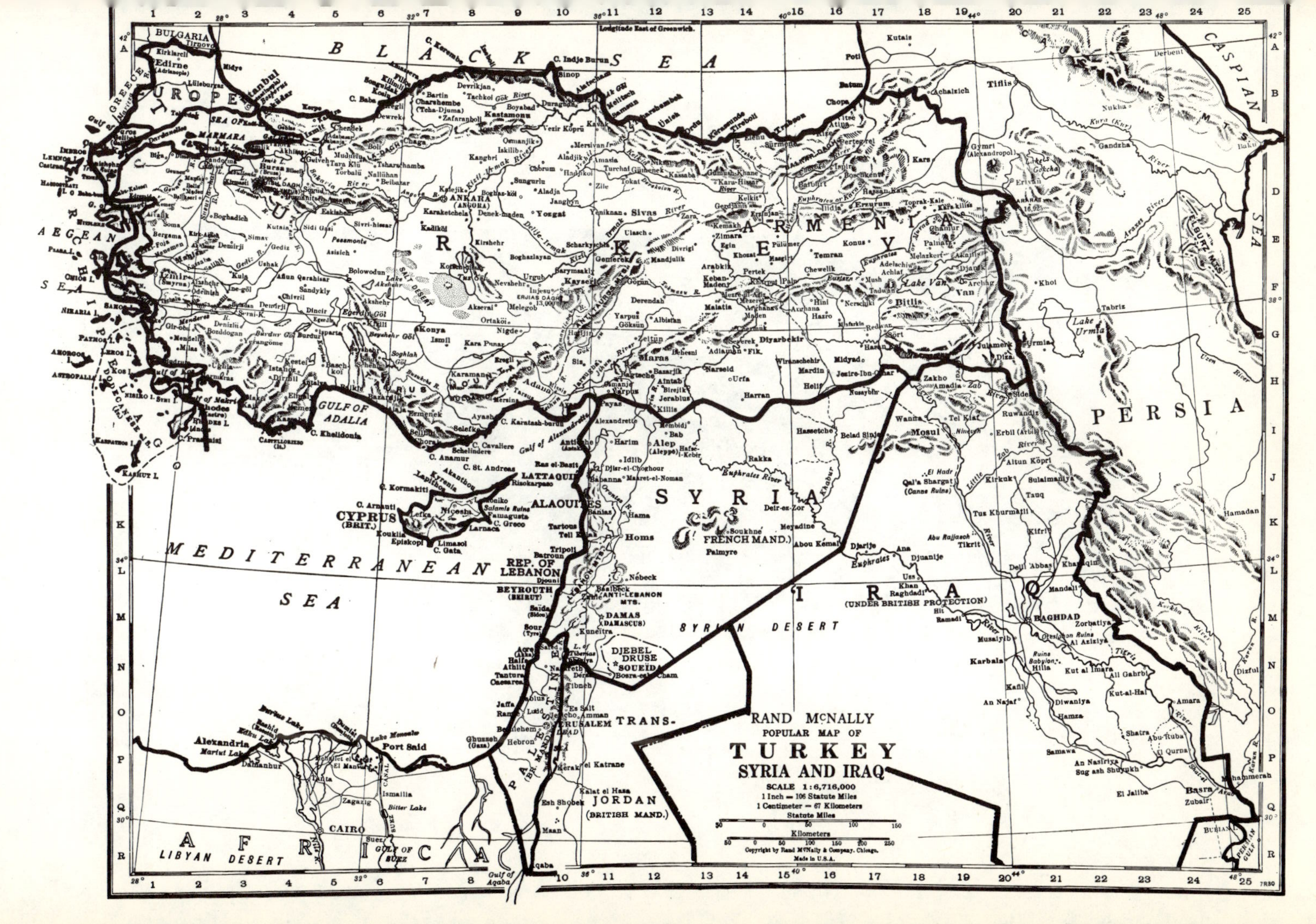

RAND McNALLY
POPULAR MAP OF
TURKEY
SYRIA AND IRAQ
SCALE 1:6,716,000
1 Inch = 106 Statute Miles
1 Centimeter = 67 Kilometers
Statute Miles
Kilometers
Copyright by Rand McNally & Company, Chicago.
Made in U.S.A.
CASPIAN SEA
BLACK SEA
MEDITERRANEAN SEA
AEGEAN SEA
PERSIA
ARMENIA
SYRIA
(FRENCH MAND.)
TURKEY
IRAQ
(UNDER BRITISH PROTECTION)
SYRIAN DESERT
LIBYAN DESERT
BULGARIA
GREECE
EUROPE
AFRICA
JORDAN
(BRITISH MAND.)
TRANS-JORDAN
PALESTINE
REP. OF LEBANON
ALAOUITES
LATTAQUIE
CYPRUS
(BRIT.)
DODECANESE
SALT DESERT
ANKARA (ANGORA)
BAGHDAD
DAMAS (DAMASCUS)
BEYROUTH (BEIRUT)
Port Said
CAIRO
Alexandria
Basra
Mosul
Aleppo
Homs
Hama
Tripoli
GULF OF ADALIA
GULF OF AQABA
GULF OF SUEZ
PERSIAN GULF
SEA OF MARMARA
SUEZ CANAL
DJEBEL DRUSE SOUEID
Palmyra
Lake Urmia
Lake Van
ELBURZ MTS.
ANTI-LEBANON MTS.

Toomas Avedisian, 1914.